The Big House

The
Big

IMAGE AND REALITY

YALE UNIVERSITY PRESS   NEW HAVEN & LONDON

House

OF THE AMERICAN PRISON

Stephen Cox

Published with assistance from the foundation established in memory of
Henry Weldon Barnes of the Class of 1882, Yale College.

Set in Janson type by Integrated Publishing Solutions.
Printed in the United States of America.

Library of Congress Cataloging-in-Publication Data

Cox, Stephen, D.
The big house : image and reality of the American prison / Stephen Cox.
p.   cm. — (Icons of america)
Includes bibliographical references and index.
ISBN 978-0-300-12419-4 (cloth : alk. paper)   1. Prisons—United States.
2. Prisoners—United States.   I. Title.
HV9469.c694 2009
365′.973—dc22   2009008329

A catalogue record for this book is available from the British Library.

This paper meets the requirements of ANSI/NISO Z39.48-1992
(Permanence of Paper).

10 9 8 7 6 5 4 3 2 1

Icons of America
Mark Crispin Miller, Series Editor

Icons of America is a series of short works written by leading scholars, critics, and writers, each of whom tells a new and innovative story about American history and culture through the lens of a single iconic individual, event, object, or cultural phenomenon.

To Mehmet Karayel

Contents

Contents

Acknowledgments

Ross Posnock, whose friendship is an honor, recommended my work to Mark Crispin Miller, who gave me the kind of encouragement that writers need. Mark, the editor of the Icons of America Series, introduced me to Jonathan Brent, my generous editor at Yale University Press, who in turn introduced me to his colleague Sarah Miller. Sarah aided my work at every stage of its journey toward publication. Dan Heaton, my manuscript editor, offered advice that was not only useful but entertaining. Library people, museum people, and prison people from many parts of America helped me when it really counted. I especially want to thank Rick Brown, Debbie French, Sergio Molina, Deb Ryman, and DeDe Short, all from the Illinois Department of Corrections; Roberta Fairburn, Debbie Hamm, and Mary Michals of the Abraham Lincoln Presidential Library; Heather Bigeck of the Joliet Area Historical Museum; Julie Meyerle of the Archives of Michigan; and Jim Blodgett, who shared with me the experiences of a lifetime in prison administration. Nathan Kantrowitz gave me the benefit of his intimate knowledge of the sociology of prisons, and particularly of Stateville Penitentiary under the old regime. Inmates, former inmates, wardens, and officers always treated me with courtesy and kindness. Joseph Ho, who knows everything about photography, gave me indispensable help with pictures. Andrew Scull showed me where I was on the right track, and where I was off on a siding. Paul Beroza and Liam Vavasour were always willing to "talk about the new book," no matter how enthusiastic or pedantic its author became.

ONE

Touring the Institution

Any list of candidates for the Great American Novel is likely to include Willa Cather's *O Pioneers!* (1913). It is a story about the trials and triumphs of a woman who knows what's right and is determined to do it. In one of the book's dramatic moments, Alexandra Bergson goes to the Nebraska State Penitentiary to visit a man who committed a crime of passion—the murder of her brother and her best friend. She goes there to forgive him.

Alexandra is a courageous person—yet the prison's ability to transform its inhabitants daunts even her. She tries not to look at the convict's "hideous" striped uniform, but she cannot stop herself from studying his "chalky gray" complexion and his close-shaved head, which gives him "a criminal look which he had not had during the trial." When the "ruddy, cheerful-looking" warden invites her to tour "the institution," she declines "with hor-ror."[1] She, and her creator, have had enough of the Big House.

Others were not so squeamish. Prisons were major tourist at-tractions. As early as 1839, Pennsylvania's Eastern Penitentiary was attracting four thousand admiring tourists a year. At about the same time, New York's Auburn Prison was being visited by more than seven thousand a year, despite the substantial admis-sion fee of twenty-five cents—in today's money, the price of a first-run movie. During the next hundred years, prisons contin-ued admitting guests and earning cash. In the first decade of the twentieth century, Atlanta's federal penitentiary was toured by up to three thousand people a day, and permanent passes were is-sued so that civilians could prowl about on any day they wanted. When a new warden arrived at Sing Sing penitentiary in 1919, he found the yard "as crowded with visitors as with prisoners. All mingled freely." He said that Sing Sing, which was just up the Hudson River from New York City, was considered "more fa-mous perhaps than the Statue of Liberty. . . . Visitors from out of town seeking 'to do the prison' are so numerous."[2]

The Kansas Industrial Reformatory voiced the common sen-timent: "Visitors are always welcome." Many institutions went out of their way to entertain the curious. Michigan's largest prison eventually excluded visitors under sixteen so that they wouldn't see "things that were not good for them," but it contin-ued selling tickets to big variety shows put on by inmates. Be-sides the paying guests, a constant stream of athletes, politicians, high school students, members of fraternities and sororities, circus performers, actors, preachers, professors, and do-gooders of all descriptions flowed through the gates.[3]

If you didn't visit a prison, you could still buy reproductions and memorabilia. You could collect decorative plates bearing the images of penitentiaries, painted in romantic colors, just like Niagara Falls or the U.S. Capitol. You could set your table with vases and cutlery depicting your favorite Big House, and accent the display with salt and pepper shakers in the form of striped-suited convicts. You could amuse your friends with model canoes and tomahawks stamped with the insignia of a state prison. You could buy some of the vast array of postcards of prisons and prison life that were produced between 1900 and 1940. You could collect them or use them as stationery: "Have been through Prison and had fine time sorry to say I am not homesick."[4] Or you could spend time with any of the thousands of prison memoirs, guides to state prisons, journalistic investigations of prison conditions, and more or less informed novels and stories about prison that gushed from the press in the nineteenth and twentieth centuries. When other media came along, you could enjoy some of the many hundreds of films, television movies, and TV series made about the Big House.

Academic literature has often treated prisons as if they were actually what many of them pretended to be: utopias of isolation and control. The followers of Michel Foucault, one of the past century's most influential writers of cultural theory, sometimes say that "what is particular about prison[s] compared to other arms of the criminal justice system—the police and the courtroom, for example—is their inaccessibility, their shrouding in secrecy."[5] On the contrary: the Big House was a shameless self-advertiser; and although many of the advertisements were misleading, it's hard to say that average Americans have ever had a much more accurate impression of what goes on in courtrooms or police stations than of what goes on in prison. Their impression of the Big House may be imperfect, but it's firm and definite. It sticks in the mind—an indelible mental image, full of interesting symbols and suggestions. It's what we mean when we use the word *icon*.

Reliable statistics about the total prison population began to be compiled in 1880. In that year, the federal census counted just over thirty thousand convicts in U.S. prisons. By 1910, when the term *Big House* was becoming part of underworld slang, the population had more than doubled.[6] By 1930 it had quadrupled, and the warden of Sing Sing could remark that there were roughly as many people in prison as there were in the U.S. Army.[7] The inmate population appeared all the more significant because it tended to be concentrated in prisons that were getting very big. Of the 120,000 American convicts, a large proportion were held in a few institutions. A third resided in the federal prisons at Leavenworth, Kansas (3,600), and Atlanta (3,100), and in the state institutions at Columbus, Ohio (4,300); San Quentin, California (4,300); Jackson, Michigan (3,800); Jefferson City, Missouri

(3,800); Joliet-Stateville, Illinois (3,100); Mansfield, Ohio (2,900); McAlester, Oklahoma (2,500); Folsom, California (2,200); Pendleton, Indiana (2,000); Michigan City, Indiana (2,000); and Chester, Illinois (2,000).[8]

Four decades earlier, only twelve prisons had housed more than 1,000 convicts each, and none more than 2,000, but more than one-third of America's convicts lived in those twelve prisons.[9] In the 1890s a really "big" prison might be something on the order of San Quentin (population 1,194), Sing Sing (1,369), New York State's reformatory at Elmira (1,396), or the Ohio Penitentiary (around 1,700); and many prisons considered "big" housed fewer than 1,000 inmates.[10] What they shared wasn't a formidable population but a formidable set of custodial and artistic styles. To some degree, this was a regional taste. Several states in the Deep South waited until the twentieth century to acquire a Big House; in those places, convicts worked on road gangs or prison farms, sometimes guarded by other convicts, without a pretense at reformatory purpose. But northern and western states invested heavily in penitentiaries. Prisons in those regions conformed to the Big House ideal: they had essentially the same gates, the same bars, the same menacing walls, the same self-confident attitude as the biggest brothers of their generation; and they expressed the same local pride. Even Kentucky, a border state, opened a "Gothic cathedral of corrections," poised atop a hill "like a giant sphinx against the sky."[11] It was part of a humanitarian governor's attempt at prison reform. Better sites, and other designs, were available, but he was willing to pay for a cathedral, and that's what he got.

The press never tired of praising the architectural authority of the Big House. "Like unto a great city viewed from a distant hilltop," wrote a reporter in a popular magazine of the 1890s, "is the mighty bastile of the State of Illinois, the world famous prison located at Joliet. . . . The massive walls and buildings tower toward the skies, so that the place can be seen for several miles from either direction." The author likes the fact that this penal "city" is run "on modern and humane principles," with every intention of reforming its inmates, but he also relishes its terrifying aesthetic effects: "The most hardened wretch shudders as he looks at those strong, gloomy walls."[12] Two generations later, a writer for another popular magazine, the kind that people bought from a rack in the drugstore, hailed Sing Sing as a place "like a medieval city . . . protected by walls and watchtowers on all sides" that was nevertheless "well-equipped" to educate convicts "for a new start" in the outside world. Indeed, Sing Sing was much more "protected" and purposeful than a real city, "where temptation lurks at every corner." Reporting on the inauguration of Georgia's new prison at Reidsville, writers for *Life* magazine, the glossiest purveyor of images to the American middle class, lauded the Roosevelt-modern building with its faux-Greek architecture as "a thing of grim beauty," noting, without much sympathy, that convicts "hate and dread" this symbol of prison progress.[13]

To observe the continuity of journalistic responses to the Big

House, we can return to Joliet, after its "mighty bastile" (which occupied only about eleven acres) had been overshadowed by the new Stateville Penitentiary, a few miles away. Stateville was now praised for its own aura of autonomy. It was "a self-sufficient city. . . . Big—everything in the prison is big." The penitentiary could also be praised as "little," in the sense of "microcosmic": "a separate little world as full of wonders as Lilliput or Brobdingnag in Swift's 'Gulliver's Travels' . . . as self-sufficient and independent of the rest of the world as most nations." The social policy of this prison nation was "the ultimate expression of [the] modern welfare state . . . which differs from the Declaration of Independence by substituting 'security' for 'liberty' as the chief aim of civilization."[14]

Nation was one metaphor for size and completeness. *City* was another. According to journalists, Michigan's biggest prison was "Just Like a Large City," with its own water and power, telephone system, industries, garage, laundry, hospital, school, theater, library, newspaper, bank, and "restaurants." Inside its "severe but not unpleasing architecture" was everything its citizens might reasonably require. The local paper was proud to announce that the prison system's herd of Holstein-Friesian cows was the "Largest in [the] World." A souvenir book sold by the penitentiary extended the compliment of bigness to modern prisons in general: "prison" had to be a "vast, complex institution," a "world within a world." Its purpose was to isolate its inhabitants from normal society, so it necessarily took on all the functions of a total "community." This concept was broadly shared. The idea of the Big House as an autonomous disciplinary world appears even in the official description of the most liberal and "open" of U.S. prisons, the California Institution for Men at Chino: "It has everything a modern city boasts, save freedom."[15] Chino was comparatively small, but it was intended to be total.

Size isn't measured simply by numbers: it's also measured by the impression of size. In 1960, when Big Houses were going out of fashion, America's convict population reached 226,000. Today it is about 1.5 million. This is roughly three times larger than the army, and about the same size as the active-duty armed forces as a whole. Yet before the prison population grew from one out of 1,600 residents of the United States (in 1880) to one out of 800 (in 1960) to one out of 200 (today), the idea and the ideal of the American prison were firmly in place.[16] Prison was a Big House, "a world of its own," complete and self-contained, unquestionably a big thing in American life. In 1957 *Life* magazine was struck by the realization that "there are as many people in prison today in the U.S. as there are living in a city the size of Tulsa, Okla."[17] That sounded like a lot, though it wasn't, in objective terms. The population of Tulsa is insignificant in relation to the total population of America. What made the number sound significant was the fact that the population was in *prison*, and that prison already had an iconic significance. Which creates a more definite and resonant image: the Big House, or Tulsa, Oklahoma? The Big House, of course.

The influence, and the intimate knowledge, of the Big House went far beyond the census figures. Big prisons have always tended to be located in small communities, places where the prison payroll has a major impact. And because prison work usually hasn't paid very well, it has often been a transient occupation—a circumstance that has multiplied the number of civilians who have had direct contact with prisons. These people may not be as articulate as professional criminologists, but that doesn't mean they have less comprehension of the subject. Combine their experience with that of the millions of people who have seen a friend or relative sent to prison, and you'll conclude that ordinary Americans have never lacked a fund of information about prison life.

The Big House—the vast, threatening, self-important American prison, the place where men were sent to be "isolated [as] on a Pacific island"—was never as isolated or as self-sustaining or even as vast as it looked; but it was the kind of enclosure that enticed curiosity and rewarded it with knowledge, entertainment, and, frequently, employment.[18] It enticed its neighbors and visitors to share its curious pride. No one mounts a souvenir of a state prison in the china cabinet without feeling pride in the prison's walls and towers. Generally speaking, the Big House was regarded as an enhancement of its community. Nineteenth-century towns competed to house the state prison in the way they competed to house the state capitol. They were overjoyed when they heard that the prison would be theirs. In 1885, when

Santa Fe, New Mexico, completed its tiny replica of an eastern Big House, the city's elite held a full-dress ball in the new building, with music furnished by an army band.[19]

In the twentieth century, Attica, New York, took "as much pride" in its penitentiary "as Niagara Falls does in its cataract, and Gettysburg its battlefield." Forty years after the construction of this "handsome" prison, called by the *New York Times* a "convicts' paradise," its inmates staged one of the nation's most destructive riots, making *Attica* a synonym for *disaster*.[20] Nevertheless, small American communities are still lobbying to get *their* prisons, and any abandoned Big House that is still in fair condition offers a source of tourist revenue to the lucky town that possesses it. The former penitentiary at Alcatraz is one of the nation's chief targets of tourism, and it is doubtful that visitors who come home wearing a shirt that says "Property of Alcatraz Federal Prison" are any less enthusiastic than the people who, four generations ago, were happy to buy soup bowls, butter dishes, and stereoscope cards celebrating the penitentiaries that interested them most.

Like other American icons, the Big House was both feeling and fact, image and reality. A brief definition of the term might read like this: "Big House: a type of penal institution that predominated in America from the mid-nineteenth to the midtwentieth century, designed to punish criminals and reform them by isolation in a totally controlled environment." But that definition, though accurate, is far too bland. The Big House was, and remains, America's notion of what a prison is supposed to be—a huge, tough, ostentatiously oppressive pile of rock, bristling with bars and towers and rules and punishments, overwhelming in its intent to intimidate. Like a literal icon, a religious picture, the Big House had both definition and complexity. It was an image composed of many images, a combination of many impressions, derived from institutions erected across the American landscape, institutions that, together, made a permanent mark on the popular imagination.

The great age of the Big House began in 1876, with the opening of New York's Elmira Reformatory, the first really large prison with a total program for the confinement and transformation of inmates. Here the idea of isolating criminals in an enormous cage converged with the idea of reforming them with "scientific" discipline. Elmira was a gigantically "beautiful" structure enclosing a minutely regulated society. Elmira-like institutions soon appeared elsewhere. Some were called prisons, others reformatories or penitentiaries; some made only a pretense at fulfilling their purported ideals; but all were loud announcements of the attempt to construct an autonomous convict world. The loudest statements came in the 1920s and 1930s, with the opening of Illinois' Stateville Penitentiary near Joliet and Michigan's new state prison at Jackson, the second of which would attain a capacity of more than five thousand men, and with the federal government's conversion of Alcatraz Island into The Rock.

By the 1960s the popularity of the Big House had faded among legislators and penologists. Smaller prisons were desired— smaller and tougher, or smaller and easier, depending on the penological theory attached to them. It was the end of the Big House as an officially favored institution. But the Big House has enjoyed a comfortable afterlife, in substance as well as symbol. Old prisons are usually too expensive to be abandoned; and although some of them have been, their images and associations have retained a life of their own. As a symbol, an idea, a key to unlocking certain potent states of mind, the Big House has proven irreplaceable.

When we talk about images and icons, we are necessarily talking about art. A natural object or an accidental event (Niagara Falls, the *Titanic*'s collision with an iceberg) can become iconic, but only because people say and do things that make it permanently impressive and resonant with meaning.[21] An icon of popular culture is something that has, in this way, been planted so deeply in the public imagination that everybody knows about it and thinks that he or she also understands its significance. A twenty-first-century comic book shows a prison bus pulling up to the Mordor-like walls and gates of an old penitentiary. The bus is full of convicts being delivered to prison. As the new inmates leave the bus, one of them says to another, "From this point on, we're basically bugs, right?"[22] The scene is so familiar, the human implications (in prison, people are transformed into "bugs") are so easy to understand, that no reader has to pause and figure them out. The imagery of prison can simply be received as it was transmitted by generations of pictures, films, and stories about the Big House. But even in its glib, comic book form, the Big House retains some of the emotional force that people started to give it long before.

Whatever else it may be, an icon is an aesthetically powerful symbol, an image with much the same power to concentrate ideas and inspire memorable emotions as a notable work of art. The Big House was the product of many motives—humanitarian enthusiasm, local pride, government job provision, and many others. One of these motives was the essentially artistic impulse to design an orderly, meaningful, deeply impressive public object.

When a Big House was under construction, critics often charged, correctly, that it was built "without careful regard to economy" or "at a needless cost." Yet they seldom doubted that a powerful image was being projected. And this wasn't mere propaganda, designed to fool outsiders. Zebulon Brockway, master of Elmira, resembled many other prison builders and managers in being stirred by the beauty of his own Big House. It looked, he said, "so much like a college or a hospital."[23]

In fact, the Big House could seldom be mistaken for anything other than a Big House. Not even the most exclusive college or hospital could match its iron gates and thirty-foot walls, its haughty sense of self-enclosure, its ambitious designs on the beings it confined. The Big House was something new, and unmistakably itself. It was America's most prominent attempt to create a separate, nonnatural world, fully stocked with people— an enormous work of living art.

A poem may be bad or good and still be considered a poem. Even a bad poem, a poem that embodies false ideas in faulty rhythms, remains a poem, and it may (at least for a while) make some of the same impressions we expect from high literary achievement. In a similar way, the Big House may be considered a success or failure as a social institution without losing its character as art. And as with other types of art, the Big House is connected to but also distinguishable from the ways in which people have interpreted it. Both the institution and the impression it has made are important, and both will be considered here—although it must be admitted that no one will ever present a full interpretation of this strange work of art, or the men who inhabited it.

I say "men" to emphasize the fact that this book is about the big picture of the American prison, not the full picture. As an institution and an icon, the Big House was always about men, not women. Women were sent to prison during the Big House period, but (then, as now) they were sent in much smaller numbers than men. Not until 1987 did the ratio of women to men rise above 1:20. Women were housed in tiny units of their own, isolated from the monumental quarters provided for the men, or they were dispatched to all-female institutions often intended to resemble "homes," "cottages," or other "family" environments. They lived in the Small House, not the Big House.[24] The condition of female felons was periodically studied in the specialized penological literature, but the general idea was to keep them out of the public gaze. For good or ill, women's prisons never became iconic.

Neither—for good or ill—did statistics about recidivism, concerns about the civil rights or educational opportunities of the convicted, or many of the other favorite topics of prison experts. Even the public's morbid interest in the death penalty seems not to have affected its concept of the Big House. After all, executions were often carried out in local jails, not prisons; and until the mid-twentieth century few victims of the death penalty were allowed much time to inhabit a prison. They went to their deaths rapidly. The death penalty had its individual iconic associations, distinct from those of the Big House. The Big House was not about death; it was about a special form of life.

This book is concerned with the idea of the Big House as a separate world, a world in which men could live that form of life—an idea that continues to assert itself in films and television shows and tourist attractions and Web sites and computer games, and conceptions (true or false) of dominance and submission.

In the next chapter we will look at the history of the Big House, and consider how such a thing might be designed. Then we'll experience daily life in the total institution. After that, we'll return to the question of how total, and how separate from the rest of society, the Big House really was. Finally, we'll examine the people who tried to change the Big House, and what happened as a result.

TWO

How to Build a Big House

Picture two lines of stone rooms built back to back, one hundred rooms in a line. Each room is seven feet long, six and a half feet high, and three and a third feet wide. Modern bathrooms and closets are larger than that. But these rooms aren't bathrooms or closets. Each is a person's complete living space, and each is fitted with an iron door and iron bars, to make sure he stays inside. Besides the inmate himself, the room contains a bunk (hinged to the wall), a water can, a wash basin, and a bucket for the occupant's waste products. Often there is more than one occupant.

Now picture twelve hundred of these compartments, stacked six stories high in one gigantic building. Each of the five upper tiers is fronted with a narrow walkway. A few feet from the walkways is a stone wall, pierced by little windows—the outer wall of the cellhouse. The first cages in this giant zoo were built in 1825.

By 1859, hundreds of them were inhabited by two men each. The cages were used until 1943.

This is Sing Sing—in population, the largest prison in early America.[1] Its contemporaries saw it as "vast." Many also regarded it as "a noble structure."[2]

Sing Sing (originally "Mount Pleasant" before it assumed an Indian place name) was built when prisons were seen as a happy alternative to the gallows, branding irons, and whipping posts that had been the traditional means of punishing crime. Strictly speaking, nothing in human history is inevitable, but if anything comes close to inevitability, it's the evolution of the penitentiary system. Imagine a world in which criminals are paraded down Fifth Avenue to be whipped in front of Rockefeller Center, a world in which the walls of Grand Central Terminal are lined with stocks and pillories. That would have been the modern world, if eighteenth-century practices had continued. In the eighteenth century, punishment was public and painful. But our world is different. Modern American civilization permits almost everything, at some time and place, except the public infliction of pain. If pain is involved in punishment, it must be merely psychic, and it must be justified both by practical ideas about control and isolation and by progressive ideas about reform. Pain takes the form of humiliation and deprivation, administered in its own special world, a world that can be praised and advertised as a special world.

Sing Sing and its immediate predecessors—Auburn Prison in western New York (opened in 1817), the Eastern or Cherry Hill

Penitentiary at Philadelphia (1829)—were imperfect approximations of the ideal. At Cherry Hill, inmates were kept in solitary confinement, in cells that were small (eighty-eight square feet), though not nearly so small as those at Sing Sing. The cells were attached to token backyards (160 square feet), where exercise was taken singly, each convict being completely isolated from contact with others.[3] Cherry Hill was a cloister, not a world. At Auburn, convicts were isolated in their cells at night but were worked together during the day. The "Auburn system" was an inspiration for many American prison practices of the nineteenth century, probably because the inmates' factory work contributed conspicuously to their upkeep. Auburn, indeed, was less a world than a factory staffed by robots-in-training.

Sing Sing was the child of Auburn. At Sing Sing, convicts labored in gangs, wrenching the walls of their prison from the limestone quarry that had determined its location. Following the rules of Auburn, they were forbidden to speak to one another. Their expectations were limited to food and a stone cell, if they obeyed orders, and a whipping if they didn't.

Yet however ridiculous it may seem, both the "Pennsylvania plan" and the "Auburn plan" proposed to reform convicts as well as punish them. The idea was a hard sell, even at the time. People who knew something about prisons (or human nature) regarded convicts at Auburn and Sing Sing as criminals who were desperate to escape from their work regime, not as citizens who were learning to better themselves. People also thought that many subjects of the Pennsylvania plan had been rendered insane by solitary confinement. These perceptions were basically correct. Prison doctors in Pennsylvania responded to criticism with statistics purporting to show that if any convicts were insane, they had been that way before they had been immured in their solitary cells, or that insanity had been temporarily contracted (especially among "colored" convicts) by indulgence in the solitary vice of masturbation.[4] But the testimony of such physicians was much less reliable than common sense. If you were locked up by yourself in an eighty-eight-square-foot cell, you would probably masturbate, and you might well become insane.

The Auburn plan had its own drawbacks. People imprisoned in an Auburn-style institution naturally preferred escape to "reformation." Conditions were brutal. Sing Sing waited fifty-two years to build a wall around itself because, so it was thought, the prison didn't need a wall; it had punishment and intimidation instead. A young Frenchman, Alexis de Tocqueville, beginning his career as America's most famous foreign visitor, noted that Sing Sing inmates were kept in their place only by the boldness and severity of their keepers. This severity manifested itself in savage punishments. Sing Sing's builder, Elam Lynds, considered the greatest penological figure of his age, regarded inmates as "coarse beings" who had only a hazy perception of "ideas, and often even sensations." His purpose was to break them, to convince them that he was strong and they were weak. In a way, he succeeded. Under his brutal leadership, Sing Sing came as close to the law of the jungle, or of Devil's Island, as any American penitentiary has ever come. Yet escapes were remarkably frequent, almost as frequent as denunciations of Sing Sing as a "modern *Gehenna*."[5] Lynd's version of the Big House did not survive; even at Sing Sing, the regime was forced to change.

The model that endured and triumphed was that of a separate but morally exemplary world, in intention, at any rate—punitive, yet also conscientiously reformative. In 1870 a national congress of prison progressives met at Cincinnati and put the ideal into words. They were much concerned with the prison as a physical object. Calling penal architecture "a matter of grave importance," they decreed that prisons should possess the most advanced systems of lighting, ventilation, and sanitation. Furthermore, "prisons of every class should be substantial structures, affording gratification by their design and material to a pure taste, but not costly or highly ornate." The congress added that institutions "of moderate size are best."[6] The bigger the Big House grew, the harder it was to govern.

Some of this advice was followed; some was not. Prisons became more and more "substantial," often exceeding anything like a "moderate size"; and aesthetic "gratification" was often a more serious consideration than either size or cost. The Big House was an architectural display, towering over the surrounding community as its largest and usually its most interesting feature. Penitentiaries were some of the first large civic institutions erected by the new states west of the Alleghenies. A four- or five-story cellhouse, protected by a stone wall encircling several city blocks, looks very big in a town where everything else is a nondescript one- or two-story something, built on land only recently cleared from the forest. A penitentiary was a status statement: this is progress; this is civilization; we have arrived.

English prison architects had specialized in geometrical fantasies, a few of which were actually rendered in brick and stone. They had also experimented with the heavy, castlelike architecture that seemed most assertive of a prison's threatening personality. Their concepts had some influence in America. Cherry Hill was an American prototype of the castlelike prison. It boasted massive walls with "medieval" towers, and beautiful neo-Norman decorative features. This was all absurdly expensive, especially in view of the fact that Cherry Hill inmates were permanently confined to their quarters and never allowed to get near the outer walls—walls that appear to have cost as much as the whole of Sing Sing.[7] Eastern was "the most extensive edifice" of any kind in the United States, and the one most capable of giving Americans an experience of "those magnificent and picturesque castles of the middle ages, which contribute to embellish the scenery of Europe." Tocqueville and his friend Gustave de Beaumont regretted that funds had been unnecessarily spent on "ornament," but this merely signified that, compared with many of their American contemporaries, these visitors had a deficient appreciation of penal art.[8]

America's prisons were seldom without an emphasis on style.

The style might be (and ordinarily was) derivative, but it was decisive, monumental, not to be forgotten. Prisons were designed to look like Egyptian temples (New Jersey State Prison at Trenton, 1836), Second Empire hôtels de ville (Cincinnati Workhouse, central structure, 1870), Greek Revival statehouses (Michigan State Prison at Jackson, 1860s), Italian villas (Michigan State Reformatory at Ionia, 1878), neoclassical palaces (Southern Illinois Penitentiary at Chester [Menard State Prison], 1880), the Tuileries (Western Penitentiary at Pittsburgh, 1881), the Pantheon (New Jersey Reformatory at Rahway, 1901), and innumerable Norman, Gothic, and crusader castles. Illinois' "castellated Gothic" institution at Joliet, opened in 1858, "excite[d] the admiration of every visitor"—according to a disgusted prison reformer, who considered this a very unfortunate thing to happen to a penitentiary.[9] But people who were bitterly critical of prisons could still defend the "beauty" of prison architecture and its ability to "vindicate" the community's "dignity, self-esteem, and sense of power."[10]

Styles changed. In the twentieth century, American prisons, including those built in the fairly recent past, were routinely deplored as "ancient."[11] This custom itself was already old. In 1872 an Indiana convict described his prison's "frowning" walls as "time-worn and blackened"—walls that had been built less than twenty years before.[12] Yet that sort of thing was a strong, though ironic, tribute to the aesthetic impact of the American penitentiary—to its determination to make itself impressive, and to its success in becoming so. Not only did it look like an ancient monument; in the minds of many people, including many "experts," it actually was ancient.

When, in the early twentieth century, new versions of the Big House were built, their architects often tried to make them look as modern as they were, or to make them look "ancient" in a more pleasant way than the Big Houses of the nineteenth century. The consequence was that they looked just as monumental as the older versions, or more so. A twentieth-century prison might have the appearance of a giant industrial plant (the new Michigan State Prison, 1925), a beaux-arts state capitol (Leavenworth Federal Penitentiary, 1897–1929), or even a palace of the early Italian Renaissance, complete with "refectory," ornamental tower, and period furniture (the Federal Penitentiary at Lewisburg, Pennsylvania, 1932). In any case, the prison was a statement of penological dignity, self-esteem, and power.

The designer of Lewisburg, Alfred Hopkins (1870–1941), was one of the most significant architects of American prisons. He was also a prison reformer who believed that when all was said and done, there was little difference between convicts and other people. Good architecture, he thought, would have its effect on both the convicts and the custodial staff, whom it might inspire to become "wise" and "tolerant." Hopkins wanted to create a world that was both aesthetically gratifying and morally useful. It is clear, however, that his first, second, and third priorities were purely aesthetic. In his mind, the architecture of the old Cherry Hill prison wasn't gloomy and oppressive (which it was); instead it was "forceful," "fitting," and even "pleasant" in its "mood."[13]

Hopkins didn't seem to notice that some price has to be paid for aesthetic effects, as for everything else. He assumed that prisons could be formidable and cheery at the same time. At Lewisburg, he kept the windows small and put bars on the inside rather than the outside, to maintain the institution's Renaissance appearance—from the outside. The inside view was different: the windows were indeed small, and the bars sticking out from them constantly reminded the inmate that he was a convict living in a prison cell. Whether despite or because of its architect's overweening self-assurance, Lewisburg was an important architectural statement; but what it said to its inmates was different from what it said to its architect.

Monumentalism had many costs. Convicts at Leavenworth took thirty-two years to complete a federal penitentiary that its architect insisted "should be as impressive as other national institutions." Leavenworth never rivaled the Lincoln Memorial, although sober observers conceded it a "tasteful grandeur." The great dome of the reformatory at Rahway, reputed to be the largest dome in the United States, surpassing that of the Capitol in Washington, cost the current equivalent of six million dollars, almost as much as the state had meant to spend on the entire institution.[14] Even a smaller prison dome than this, used as a set in a television melodrama (*Doing Life*, 1986), creates an unforgettable image of power and subjugation, as one watches the lines of little numbered convicts snake beneath its artificial sky.

In some sense, the dome at Rahway may have been worth the cost. But prisons were much more than images. For hundreds of thousands of men, they were realities in which they had to live. So let your own imagination work. Imagine that you are commissioned to design a Big House. How will you do it—and still get the realities right?

Your first challenge is obvious: keep the inmates from escaping. The logical place to start, the place from which Big House architecture almost always started, is the prison wall. You should make it about thirty feet high, so that normal ladders won't go over it. A wall of that size makes a big show for passing tourists, who will regard it as impregnable. But don't be fooled by your own architecture. No wall stands on its own. Inmates can always find a way to defeat it, unless every segment is guarded, day and night. Guard towers must be added to your plan, positioned so that any convict who tries to escape can be seen, and shot, from one or more of them. And because the tower guards will be armed, their posts must be unreachable from any point inside the walls; they must be entered only from the outside. The worst thing that can happen is for inmates to attack a guard and take his gun. For this reason—contrary to what one sees in some Big House movies —officers on routine duty should be armed with nothing more than clubs or canes, as they often were in the nineteenth century; and even these weapons should probably be prohibited. In the ordinary course of events, weapons don't control convicts; convicts are controlled by personal authority.

More about that later. Let's return to the architectural framework, the perimeter wall. You must design at least two openings: one for people, one for heavy equipment and supplies delivered by rail or truck. Every entrance for bulk goods must be heavily fortified, to keep convicts from getting civilian accomplices to ram the gates and let them out. Every entrance of any kind must have an inner and an outer gate, with a standing rule against opening them simultaneously. The powerhouse should be located outside the wall, to keep contraband from being smuggled in with the fuel. This means, however, that power lines must be extended from the outside to the inside, entailing piercings of the wall, which may be exploited by inmate escape artists. A "total" institution is a very complicated place. Strength in one area becomes weakness in another.

The most important thing is to manage the inmates' motions and minimize their opportunities of being alone and unobserved. The usual method is to put them in cells walled with stone, steel, or concrete, and to face the cells with bars, so that keepers, prowling the galleries, can see what's going on inside. It's best to keep inmates away from windows, and the usual way to do this is to follow the Auburn and Sing Sing model: build two parallel blocks of cells, four to six stories high, place them back to back at the center of the cellhouse, and separate them from its outer walls and windows by several yards of empty space. This will keep the convicts from reaching the windows and loosening the bars, and it will allow the cellhouses to be used, if you wish, as part of the prison's perimeter wall. That will save money.

Money can also be saved by making the cells as small as possible. And the smaller the cell, the easier it is to see into. A typical cell size in the late nineteenth and early twentieth centuries was five by seven feet, although slightly larger sizes (six by nine, for example) were also in use. By 1900, brick or stone cell walls were giving way to concrete and to space-conserving, escape-resistant sheets of iron or steel. A company that won an award of merit at the Chicago World's Fair in 1893 for its work in cell construction declared that no "intelligent" person "in this age" would construct cells of anything but steel.[15] Now it was possible to spend one's life in an all-steel cage, set in a rack of hundreds of identical all-steel cages.

A typical cellhouse, 200 feet long, 60 feet wide, and 50 feet high, might contain 300 cells, 150 in each block, 30 on each tier. And many more than 300 men could be crammed inside those 300 cells. No warden wanted to house more than one inmate in a cell, thus inciting noise and plots and homosexual relationships, but growing populations forced most of them to "double cell" or even "triple cell" their inmates. The Ohio Reformatory at Mansfield had a cellhouse able to hold 1,210 men in two-man cages. Stateville's Cellhouse B, 444 feet long, contained 580 cages and 1,300 men.[16]

The difficulty of finding places to put people was small, however, compared with the difficulty of guarding them once they were there. In some prisons, large numbers of men were locked in their cells virtually all day, every day, but that didn't solve the security problem. Locking a man up doesn't keep him from sending messages, running illicit businesses, using drugs, producing liquor, making weapons, or sawing through the bars and escaping. Inmates need to be counted several times a day; they need frequent "shake-downs," of both their cells and their bodies; even the bars of their cells need to be whacked with a stick to make sure they haven't been cut or loosened. All this takes time, and therefore money.

So does any attempt just to observe the inmates. In a normal cellblock, there is no efficient way of doing so. Tall, steep tiers of steel cages are good at inducing vertigo, and they have a tremendously intimidating effect; but their sight lines aren't good for watching the men inside. Guards on a tier can't see to the back of cells that they aren't standing in front of. Guards on the first-floor pavement, the "base" or "flag," can't see anything but a blur of the upper floors. One solution is to suspend a catwalk from the wall opposite the cells, with officers patrolling it; but officers cost money, and they still won't be able to see to the back of any more than a few cells at a time. In a typical cellhouse, the lines of barred doors stretch for five city blocks, often with only four officers to watch them. What if one or two of them turn up sick?

And a Big House is larger than its cellblocks. To the degree that it actually constitutes its own separate world, it must include all the essentials of a world. It must have kitchens and laundries and shops and offices and warehouses; it must have a chapel and a power plant and a bathhouse. It must have a place for isolation and punishment, a prison within the prison. That last feature can be provided by building a special punishment block, by dedicating part of a normal block to isolation cells, or by installing some punishment cells in the basement—literally, "the hole." But the second-most-important structure, after the cellhouses, is the mess hall, and this presents particular hazards and temptations.

If you are an ordinary Big House architect, you will want to put the mess hall in the most prominent place in the prison, and you will want to make it large enough to seat the entire body of inmates. You will design a single, vast, open space with a cathedral-like ceiling and Goliath-size doors. You will create an expanse that dwarfs the lines of narrow benches and the convicts filing in to eat at them. In the Big House, more isn't just more, it's gigantic; and less isn't just less, it's tiny and miserable. The vast mess hall fulfills the demands of the Big House aesthetic, which insists on combining that kind of More with that kind of Less.

Whether it fulfills the demands of practicality is another question. Mess halls are the most dangerous places in any prison. They are places where a few guards are lost in an ocean of convicts. Any wave of discontent, any unhappiness with the food, any questioning of a guard's authority can produce a riot. Big mess halls are big risks.

Other expedients besides the grand mess hall have always been possible. At the Illinois State Prison during the 1880s, food was dished out in the cellblocks and eaten in the cells.[17] This experiment was messy and inconvenient, but it was tried in a significant number of institutions during the last decades of the nineteenth century.[18] One can also arrange a series of smaller mess halls around a central kitchen, a plan that is sometimes used today. In the 1920s Sing Sing created a "commissary" involving four such dining rooms. Ideas like that are expensive, but so were big mess halls, which often enclosed a volume of more than two hundred thousand cubic feet. San Quentin's mess hall, the largest in the nation, enclosed about one million cubic feet and seated 4,275 convicts. The grandeur of its architectural aspirations is indicated by the fact that it was built when the prison's population was only 1,900. Despite the costs and dangers, the magnificent mess hall was the design of choice throughout the Big House period. It made almost as strong an impression as the gargantuan cellhouse or the cyclopean wall, and was an important source of statistical pride. The fact that Stateville's mess hall seated thousands was an assurance that the place was a "model prison of the world."[19]

But how should one arrange the various buildings in one's model prison? A popular nineteenth-century idea was to make them radiate from a common control point—a rotunda opening onto two or more cellhouses, the guards' hall, the warden's office, and maybe the mess hall as well. The disadvantage was that only a few large buildings could adjoin a central structure, unless the structure itself became prohibitively large. The other buildings had to be sited independently, somewhere out back, with space allotted for a "yard" through which inmates could walk from their cells to the shops or bathhouse or laundry. Unfortunately, inmates are hard to supervise once they're outside, wandering across the yard or through a maze of masonry.

A leading problem of the Big House was its success as a growth industry. As the prison population increased, new bunks were added to old cells, and new buildings to old penitentiaries. Nineteenth-century prisons needed to be located near railroads or streetcars, hence in towns; but the towns grew up around them, and prison walls weren't easy to extend. Expansion had to happen within the walls, and it usually happened without the benefit of long-range planning. Prison officials were almost always political appointees, and politics was always in flux. When a state legislature appropriated money for a new building, the current warden often simply decided, "Might as well put it *there*." The result was a jumble of buildings that inmates were able to convert into their own private worlds. A convict at the Maine state prison considered it common knowledge that homosexual inmates could be alone with one another "in such places as the bathroom [bathhouse], salt-pork cellar, Sherm's shack, the cannery, and perhaps the laundry."[20] That's a lot of places, whatever "Sherm's shack" may have been.

Yet however well you plan your prison, security problems multiply as soon as the inmates are let out of their cells—and large numbers of them have to be let out, every day, not just to work off energy that might otherwise explode but also to run the institution. No large prison has ever had anything like enough civilian employees to do its daily work. Only in very expensive super–maximum security units can every inmate be put in cuffs and shackles whenever he is out of his cell, and "supermax" is largely a creation of the late twentieth century. There will even be convicts—maintenance men, the warden's driver, the trusties who work the prison farm—who need to be allowed out of the gates. The best practice is to house as many of them as possible in outside barracks, so they will have no occasion to go back and forth, trailing contraband and illicit news, and to find some means of keeping the convicts who live inside the wall under tight supervision when they leave their blocks.

"Tight," however, cannot mean "complete." An alternative to shackling the inmates is to march them in close formation every-where they need to go. But what happens after they reach their destinations? Who will ensure that the two hundred men in the shoe factory or the fifteen hundred men in the mess hall won't get out of control? The answer is: the same small squad of officers who try to patrol the blocks. And close-order marching is practical only with large gangs of men. The clerks on their way to work in the warden's office, the "runners" who carry the captain's messages, the guys who shovel the snow off the path to the mess hall—at some point, these men will be on their own.

Guards stationed on the walls can control, to some extent, the inmates they can see. They can shoot them if they try to escape or try to kill someone. But the larger the prison, the harder it is to control or even see very far into it. Serious riots in the Big House were probably never quelled merely by shooting from the walls. Even a well-trained rifleman can take action only against visible escape attempts and nearby threats to life and limb. He may be able to stop a disturbance, if he can see it, with a well-aimed intimidation shot, but insurgencies are something different.

In 1971 Attica was a secure-looking prison with a control point at the center and enclosed passages running out from it to the cellhouses, which provided a perimeter for the institution's four yards. But when inmates in one of the passages rioted, they had little trouble breaking through a defective gate in the control area and taking the keys that were kept there. The riot spread rapidly through the institution. Inmates took hostages and held much of the prison for several days. Attica was very much harder to recapture than it had been to capture. The insurgents were finally routed by state police and corrections officers firing from the walls and storming the interior—killing, in the process, twenty-nine convicts and ten hostages. Lack of training and organization was largely responsible for the catastrophe, but the imposing architecture of the Big House also did its part.[21]

Attica's highly unified and centralized plan was one attempt at solving the problem of controlling convict movement. Another approach, common in the mid-twentieth century, was the "telephone pole" design. In this plan, cellhouses, administrative units, shops, and so forth were built in parallel, like so many concrete dominoes, connected by a wide, high-visibility corridor—a secure area in which inmates could be watched and disciplined as they were channeled from one part of the institution to another. The yard, unencumbered by stray, unattached buildings, could be restricted to specialized recreational and maintenance uses; and the prison could expand, if necessary, by lengthening the security corridor and connecting more buildings to it.

But every solution creates another problem. In a telephone pole prison, inmates may have difficulty escaping from their designated channels, but so will their guards, if the inmates ever turn on them. The longer the central corridor extends, the harder it is to control. Inmates' movements can be monitored from guard stations along the way, but the stations have to be impregnably fortified and possessed of quick communications with security forces in remote areas of the structure. In 1956 New Mexico opened a penitentiary that the state governor proclaimed to be one of "the most advanced correctional institutions in the world." It was designed in the telephone-pole style. In 1980 inmates in one part of the prison captured their guards before they could use their radios to summon help, then ran down the corridor and applied steel pipes to the control center. Its windows were bulletproof but not pipe-proof. The rioters broke in, as they had at Attica, seized the prison's key collection and riot-suppression weapons, and invaded the rest of the institution. They beat, shot, stabbed, burned, and hacked to death at least thirty-three inmates, some of them prison enemies, others guilty only of being in the wrong place when the death squads came through.[22] Again, official incompetence played a part, but so did prison architecture.

Another architectural scheme needs to be noticed, that of Stateville Penitentiary. Stateville was one of many prisons built in the automobile age, when they could be sited in rural areas, now accessible by car. These locations provided room for architectural experiments. But Stateville was unique: it was the only American version of the most famous design in prison history, the "panopticon" or all-seeing institution of Jeremy Bentham. Bentham (1748–1832), philosopher, humanitarian, and enthusiast for improvement and reform, became addicted to fantasies of the perfect prison. His favorite concept was a round cellhouse with observation posts at the center, from which every inmate (and every guard) could be spied on at any time, ensuring complete control. Bentham was interested in virtue and reformation, not punishment per se; and he thought his institution was the way to obtain these things. Yet as he relentlessly elaborated the plans of the imaginary prison, another motive appeared to predominate—the artist's fervent appreciation of his artistry. A perceptive critic has called Bentham's prison an "artificial universe," a phrase that Bentham would have taken as a compliment. So large was his artistic ambition that he regarded the panopticon as a model for progressive social institutions in general.[23]

Bentham's fantasies were almost forgotten until the late twentieth century, when Michel Foucault resurrected them, seeing in Bentham's Big House an icon of modern Western society—a society in which, he suggested, power is exerted through constant social surveillance.[24] In other words, Foucault took the most advanced claims of Bentham, and of other Big House enthusiasts, and accepted them as true. He saw prison as both the image and the reality of a total world, a society that, while very distant from the ideal (as he saw it), actually worked. But there was one place where Bentham's ideas had been taken seriously, early in the century—the architectural firm of Zimmerman, Saxe & Zimmerman, builders of Stateville. Zimmerman and company were confident in their ability to create an artificial universe such as Bentham had in mind; and, like Bentham, they seem to have been as strongly motivated to create a distinctive work of art as they were to manage and reform the convicts who lived inside it.

Alfred Hopkins, perhaps envious of the Chicago architects' achievement, charged that Illinois "wanted to startle the world with its conception of the perfect penological structure."[25] His statement was exaggerated, but not by much. Stateville, located on a featureless prairie an hour's drive west of Chicago, was an exercise in ideal architectural proportions. An area of sixty-four acres was staked out and enclosed by thirty-three-foot walls. The security area occupied a rectangle with sides in the ratio of 1:1.5. The area bounded by the side walls, the administration building, and the service yard was a great square, enclosing another rectangle, dominated by the cellhouses; this rectangle, in turn, was centered on a circular mess hall, two hundred feet in diameter, the hub of the institution—a penologically perilous but aesthetically satisfying exercise in big art.

The enormous room was a panopticon, the center of which was a fortified observation tower. The mess hall was designed to feed two thousand inmates at a shift. A mass of people that size is very hard to monitor and control, even when everyone is seated on a bench facing the guard tower and wearing a convict number on his back; but the designers didn't allow themselves to become preoccupied with the danger of riots. They encircled the mess hall with a wide corridor from which additional corridors pointed outward, like the spokes of a wheel, to other parts of the penitentiary. One led to the imposing administration building; eight others (as originally planned) reached out to eight circular cellhouses, arranged symmetrically around the mess hall—each one a panopticon, five hundred feet in circumference, four stories high, with an elevated command post at the center. The 248 cells arranged around the circumference were painted light green, a shade "selected in accord with the psychology of color." A massive skylight was "astronomically calculated" to guarantee that no cell received less than two hours of sunlight a day.[26]

Stateville was the perfection of geometrical art, and the effect was fascinating—immense, yet intricate. "Except for the steel guard tower in the center," Chicago journalists observed, "the interior of a circular cellhouse looks something like a European opera house as viewed from the stage"—an artificial universe, indeed.[27] From the guard tower, an endlessly complicated human drama could be observed, the spectacle of a vast, closely synchronized subjection to an architectural ideal. Describing the inmates' return to their cellhouses, a liberal opponent of prisons succumbed to the aesthetic spell:

> The men keep coming in through the ground-floor gate. They climb the steps just inside it, their heavy shoes clattering on the iron steps. From the floor they can be seen splitting off in lines onto the concrete galleries, others zigzagging higher and higher, emerging on the topmost, or fourth, gallery under the roof; and then walking along the galleries to their cells, still in lines, blue uniforms moving dully against bars; those on the second gallery moving clockwise, those on the third moving counterclockwise, those on the top moving clockwise, like great spinning human wheels. As each man reaches his cell, he goes into it and shuts the door. And now the last man comes through the gate and the gate shuts with a heavy clang. They are all in their cells, 600-odd men in one building, and now the keeper in the tower throws some levers and the cell doors are locked.[28]

The only comparable spectacle was a military parade or totalitarian political demonstration, but those were visions of mobilized might, not of choreographed surrender.

The plan for eight panopticons was superseded in 1930, a year of economic hardship in which cost was more important than artistic design. The new plan combined four panopticons with one of the nation's largest rectangular cellblocks, the mammoth cellhouse B—another instance of theatrical penology, but cheaper to build than its equivalent in "opera houses." Regardless of this deviation, the completed Stateville looked like a total world— meticulously designed, heavily populated, and fully equipped with the insignia of present, past, and future. Its walls and towers, powerhouse and shops and cellhouses, were streamlined modern structures, suggesting the World of Tomorrow; but its administration building recalled the style of the Italian Renaissance, with sumptuous lobbies, a fine marble staircase, and elegant decorations in wood. In a more apposite allusion to the past, the concrete walls of the hub corridor mimicked the irregular stonework of a dungeon. Stateville presented itself as an icon of all prisons, a union of ancient privation with twentieth-century efficiency and pride.

There was one neglected area. Stateville's structures were meticulously planned, but no one seems to have thought about the aesthetics of its yard. Perhaps the mathematics of the buildings was regarded as sufficiently gratifying; compared with them, the yard was unorganized, meaningless space. It was left to Joseph Ragen, warden in the 1940s and 1950s, to bring the yard under artistic control. He converted much of it into a series of gardens, with flagstone walks, banks of flowers, lily ponds, and statues of boys-with-dogs, fishing in the ponds—a museum of horticultural kitsch. The gardens were created and maintained by inmate labor, but ordinary inmates, whose exercise facilities were described as "large bare cindered area[s] . . . bounded by a wire fence," had to view them from a distance.[29] Nothing was permitted to mar the warden's masterpiece.

As we shall see, great cunning and dedication were needed to operate an institution built in accordance with Stateville's enormous, strangely beautiful plan. The circular cellhouses worked much better than professional penologists have usually acknowledged. It is true that the guards stationed in their towers at the center of Stateville's panopticons were watched by the convicts, even while the guards were watching them (a change from Bentham's system, which went to ridiculous lengths to keep convicts from knowing when they were being watched), but the best the convicts could hope for was to commit an infraction quickly, when a guard turned his back. And Stateville was one prison in which guards at a single post could actually see all the way into every compartment of a cellhouse. Nevertheless, there were problems, beginning with Stateville's outer wall. Though it was adorned with guard towers at regular intervals, the space it enclosed was too big. Guards couldn't see far enough into that space to control the inmates. The sheer number of people imprisoned in Stateville's great rectangles was enough to discourage almost anyone who wanted to manage them.

Using examples like this, twentieth-century reformers habitually denounced American prisons as too large to be competently run. Their objections were understandable, yet they had little impact. The firm that designed Stateville went on to build a prison at Graterford, Pennsylvania, with walls enclosing virtually the same area as Stateville's. Prisons seemed so intent on getting big that, according to rumor, Stateville, Graterford, and the new penitentiary at Jackson, Michigan, were competing to be known as the Biggest Big House: "state pride" was at stake, even though the prison yards were known to be "far too large for proper supervision" and the buildings cost, by today's valuation, at least fifty thousand dollars per inmate.[30]

The rumor was unsubstantiated. Jackson's construction history shows that the prison simply *grew* in response to the Prohibition crime wave, the availability of state funds for political patronage, and the site visits of an energetic state governor, visits that sometimes resulted in on-the-spot decisions to tear down the wall and make the prison larger. Yet while interstate competition doesn't appear to have been an important motive, emotions did get involved, both during and after construction. According to a report prepared for the next governor of Michigan, even critics of Jackson's cost and ostentation thought the prison should be "admired" as "a beautiful piece of work." Locally issued postcards acclaimed it as "second to none anywhere."[31]

But the ultimate exemplar of the Big House ideal wasn't big at all in its number of inhabitants; it was big in more significant ways—psychological and aesthetic. This is Alcatraz, the most iconic of all Big Houses, a place where the arts of incarceration were displayed more clearly and conspicuously than anywhere else in the world. Alcatraz confined only about three hundred men, yet it was meant to seem Big, and it did.[32] Hunched on a dismal rock in the middle of San Francisco Bay, inescapably visible from the city's best neighborhoods, Alcatraz was a single massive cellhouse buttressed by a haughty white warden's residence and a set of surly gray industrial buildings. It had been a fort, then an army prison. In 1933 the purportedly escape-proof island was selected as the site for a new effort at prison reform. From that point on, the Rock became, for much of the American populace, the symbol of all that a prison should be. The great goal of prison reformers was "classification," the separation of "hardened criminals" from those less hardened. Now the hardest criminals in the federal prison system would be transported to fortress Alcatraz, where they would be disciplined by iron rules and guarded from escape by the waters of the Pacific Ocean.

Public relations also played a role. The public imagination was focused on gangsters, such as Chicago's Al Capone, and was gratified when Capone was sent to Alcatraz—though he spent only four years on the island (where the average stay was less than six years).[33] Then he was removed to another prison, after manifesting symptoms of dementia—a condition brought on by syphilis, not by the rigors of confinement. In fact, much of the prison's population consisted of convicts who might well have been managed in other institutions. Time on the Rock did keep criminals like Capone out of most forms of trouble, but other prisons could have done the same, if they had solved some vexing, though elementary, problems of security—preventing escapes, breaking up conspiracies and rackets, and disrupting communications with outside "businesses": in short, guarding their prisoners. Alcatraz was a strict (in some ways overly strict) institution, but its regime could have been reproduced with as much ease, or difficulty, in high-security units of prisons elsewhere in the country. Yet after more than a century of trying, the Big House still wasn't dependably secure. Apparently, all the resources of the federal government had to be concentrated on a few hundred men, marooned on a desert island, before adequate security was at last achieved.

The existence of Alcatraz indicated that there were other purposes for prison building besides security. Some of these purposes were simply iconic. The mission of Alcatraz was to symbolize the might of the federal government, to provide a concrete illustration of the government's power to make punishment certain, severe, and humiliatingly democratic. Like the other Alcatraz cons, Al Capone had to obey all the rules laid down by his $3,162-a-year keepers. He would speak only when speech was "essential or unavoidable." He would swab the floors and handle the dirty laundry. He would learn the primary law of prison: "You are entitled to food, clothing, shelter and medical attention. Anything else that you get is a privilege."[34] That was the view from Washington. Capone and his fellow convicts came to understand that view. Whether they learned anything else is another question. But Alcatraz, the best known Big House, varied ironically from the others: it did not even promise to reform its inmates.

Alcatraz closed in 1963. The government had always found it tremendously expensive to run a prison on an island where all personnel and supplies, including water, had to be shipped in. And it hadn't taken long for the salt winds of San Francisco Bay to compromise the prison's allegedly impregnable walls. The last inhabitants of Alcatraz were transferred to a new penitentiary in Illinois, built in a bland post–Big House style. If there was an end of the Big House era, this was it. The icon was no longer worth the cost of maintaining it.

Much of what I've said so far has presented a discouraging view of the problems of designing a prison capable of living up to the reputation of the Big House as a securely self-enclosed environment. But those problems were much less discouraging than the problem of living in a Big House.

THREE

Your Life as a Convict

You stood before a judge and were sentenced to prison. Then you were shackled to other convicts and taken to a train, guarded by sheriff's deputies. If there were enough of you in the "fish line," the "chain" of new prisoners, you were put on a special railway car with bars on the windows. If not, you had to ride in a regular coach and endure the stares and smiles of the other passengers. When the train stopped, you were marched through the station to a prison wagon waiting on the street. You were locked in the back of the wagon and driven to your new home.

That's how it would happen if you lived in the late nineteenth century. If you lived in the twentieth, you and your fellow convicts were probably transported to prison in a police car or a corrections department bus. But however you got there, you will never forget your first sight of the Big House, looming up behind the roofs and chimneys of an unfamiliar town—a giant's toybox of walls and towers, unmistakably your destination.

The sheriff's men pull you out of the vehicle and lead you up a flight of stone steps. You enter a room where another uniformed figure signs a receipt for the merchandise, which is you. Your shackles are removed, the sheriff's deputies depart, and you are led through a steel gate into the first of the storeroomlike spaces where you will be processed into the institution. Convicts call this "dressing in."

It's here that you start getting acquainted with your convict number, which first appears on a signboard hanging from your neck while your photographs are taken. From now on, those four, five, or six digits will be you. Convict cameramen often have a sense of humor. At the Iowa State Prison, one of them made an amusing picture story out of the processing of a young man named Prine. It shows Prine, wearing a white shirt, a tie, and his convict number, sitting for his photo. A flash of lightning appears behind him, spiking toward his head. The caption says: "This 10-year sentence—to trade his name for a number—all this has hit Prine like a bolt of blue lightning!"[1] Yes, no matter how many times you've heard of "mugshots" or how many cartoons you've seen of convicts wearing numbers, this part of your initiation will probably hit you like a bolt of lightning.

After your pictures, it's time to strip. You take off your clothes and stand in front of a guard, who tells you to bend and spread. This, for some men, is the most embarrassing moment of their lives. Following his search of your anus, the guard proceeds to your other cavities—ears, armpits, mouth. Then he seats you on a stool and an inmate barber shaves you bald. A stiff brush sweeps the remains of your hair into a wastebasket, and you're ready to be walked, naked and hairless, to a line of communal bathtubs or a showerhead where you huddle with the other new convicts for two or three minutes under a tepid stream. When you're finished, somebody dips a stick into a pail of blue slime and spreads it over your private parts. This is lice prevention.[2]

Now you've reached the place where you dress in your convict clothes (or, as the newspapers always say, "don" your convict "garb"). At the clothing counter, a convict demands your sizes, then issues you whatever sizes he wants to issue. One cap, one coat, two shirts, two pairs of trousers, two or three thick suits of underwear, two or three pairs of socks, one pair of high-topped work shoes: this is your wardrobe, perhaps for the rest of your life. While you watch, your number is stamped in black on your new clothes. As you pull on the bulky uniform, smelling of new ink, you begin to understand prison life on a deeper level: "Nearly all the men have an air as if they despised these clothes and suffered within them."[3] But for the first time you look like what you are, a convict.

If you come to prison sometime around 1900, you will be taken to the Bertillon Room, where measurements of the various parts of your body will be made, using a method of identification recently devised by the French "anthrometrician" Alphonse

Bertillon. If you arrive sometime after World War I, your finger-prints will be taken instead. A final record of your identity will be made: a second set of mugshots, recording your transformation from a man in respectable civilian clothing, the clothing you wore to court, into something with a bald head and a convict suit. The process of transforming and numerically identifying you is interesting enough to other people to occupy the covers of na-tional magazines.[4]

Next is your interview with the deputy warden, or perhaps the warden himself. This official explains to you that "the convicts are convicts, the guards guards," and assures you that trouble awaits "any convicts who fail to understand the difference."[5] You say "yes, sir" several times, and a guard leads you out of the office. Some basic supplies are issued—blanket, washcloth, toothbrush, soap, a book of rules—and you're delivered to your cell. It may be located in a block directly connected with the administration building, or it may be some distance away. In either case, your journey through the institution will not prepare you for what happens when the steel door opens and you find yourself inside the cellhouse. First there's the smell: "fetid air reminiscent of old socks and sweat and disinfectant," mixed with "the odor of worn metal."[6] Then there's the sight: a cliff of numbered cages looming above you, five or six stories tall. One of these cages is for you.

Before negotiating the narrow staircase that takes you to your tier, you may be lectured by an officer about keeping your quar-ters tidy. He may show you a bunk with a sign attached: "MAKE

YOUR BED SAME AS SAMPLE."[7] This lesson over, he marches you up the iron stairs, your heavy new shoes clomping uncomfortably on every step, your cell supplies and extra uniforms wobbling in your arms. "Left!" he says, and you're stomping along an iron catwalk with a drop-off of forty feet on one side and a line of bars on the other. You try not to look at what's behind the bars. "In here!" he says, and one set of bars slides back. You enter, and he locks you in—if you're lucky, alone.

Most convicts have one or two roommates. In a really modern prison, such as Stateville, the dimensions of your cell will be more generous than they were in Sing Sing, but you may still have to share your cell with two other men. In that case, the distance between the top of your nose and the bottom of the next bunk up will be only about one foot.[8] You hope that your cellies will have certain desirable characteristics: neatness, cleanliness, civility, ordinary physical strength, intransigent heterosexuality. In the Big House, this combination of qualities is often in short supply.

If you are sent to a progressive, mid-twentieth-century prison, you may be celled for a while in "isolation" or "seg" (segregation) while "diagnostic" reports are prepared on you. You will sit on the other side of the desk from a prison psychologist or sociologist and answer his questions so that he can recommend something about your "classification" (the degree of restraint you need) and your assignment to either a job or idleness. But soon you will be remanded to "population," and your daily routine will begin.

You spend your nights listening to the snores, mutterings, and insane ramblings of your neighbors. You wake at dawn to a bell or bugle. You are allowed a few minutes to wash your face and use the toilet, or the bucket, in your cell. There's a history to this, which you may not know. During much of the nineteenth century, inmates were left at night with a can of drinking water and a lidded pail for their urine and feces. They carried their "honey pots" out in the morning and emptied them into an open sewer. Other inmates washed the buckets down, and their owners retrieved them while returning to their cells. Toilets and running water became popular in the 1880s, although the bucket system endured through the 1920s at Sing Sing, and through the 1950s at the Montana State Prison.[9] Eventually all prisons acquired indoor plumbing. Yet emptying one's bowels on a seatless toilet in the corner of a tiny cell, with cellmates watching or trying not to watch, remained one of the worst features of the Big House. "Fourteen hours with the same man, or men," exclaimed a veteran convict. "It is a marvel that they don't kill each other. . . . I've often thought during my quarter century of confinement that having a bowel movement in private would be the world's finest luxury."[10]

You attend, as best you can, to your bodily functions; then you put on your uniform and stand at the bars of your cell to be counted. You will stand there again several times during the day. Each time, all activity will cease until the count is finished. When the morning tally is verified, a lever is thrown somewhere below you, the gate of your cage unlocks, and you stand out on the gallery and start your march to the mess hall.

If you are a convict in an old-fashioned prison, this and all other large population movements are conducted in "lockstep" with ten, twenty, or fifty other men. Each convict fits his body to that of the convict in front of him and "locks" himself in position by gripping the front man's shoulder with his right hand. Then the mass shuffles forward, legs pumping in unison, heads slanted sideways toward the officer in charge. Observers found the lockstep disturbing and fascinating: "The line looks like a great, many-legged reptile. . . . The resemblance . . . to some great serpent is most striking, and even revolting."[11] This Big House custom was as tenacious as it was picturesque. Although it was abolished in many prisons during the late nineteenth century, including Sing Sing in 1900, it lasted another five decades in Ohio. If you have strange feelings about marching with your body locked to the bodies of other men, you aren't alone: one of the reasons why the lockstep was finally eliminated was its tendency to arouse homosexual desires.[12]

Dining in the mess hall will not be cheerful. You will be seated on a stool or backless bench, jammed shoulder to shoulder with hundreds or thousands of other men lined up with mathematical rigidity, all facing one way, with guards staring back at them. The food is cheap and ugly, and sometimes disgusting, although, for better or worse, there's usually plenty of it. You can eat all you want, in the fifteen or twenty minutes you're given to eat. The rule is: take all you like, but don't let anything go to waste. If you fail to clean your plate, you will be punished.

You aren't trusted with a knife or fork. You aren't trusted with pepper: you might save it up and use it to blind a guard. Your equipment is a spoon, a tin plate, and perhaps a tin cup, stamped with your number, that can be hitched to your trousers. Until the 1940s many prisons forbade any conversation in the mess hall. In a place like that, you'll need to signal silently to the convict waiter if you want more bread. The only sounds in the room will be the shuffling of the waiters' feet and the noise of mastication. You will probably agree with one of the college types who keep coming around to "study" you: "The sight of 1,200 men stoically eating in silence is gruesome."[13]

After your breakfast you're marched back to your cellhouse for another count and then, if you're fortunate, to a work assignment. Almost any kind of work is better than rotting in your cell. Your job may be sweeping a floor or sweating in a quarry; it may be working in a factory that makes furniture or canned goods or binder twine. Around noon, you're marched to the mess hall again, then returned to your cell or job. In late afternoon you eat the last meal of the day. If the sun is still up, you may be permitted some exercise in the yard before being celled for the night. Once celled, you stand at your bars for a count. One or more counts will be taken while you're asleep. The light in your cell goes out at 9 P.M., but the range lights on the walkway stay on. "It's somewhat hard to explain to a new man," a convict wrote, "that as long as he was in prison he would never know darkness or silence."[14]

So much for your weekday schedule. On weekends, you may attend a service in the chapel. You may be marched to the inmate store or "commissary" to buy cigarettes or a box of candy with the small amounts of prison scrip you are allowed. You may be taken to the auditorium to see a movie. From the 1920s on, most prisons offer weekly film presentations. While it's true that if trouble doesn't start in the mess hall, it will probably start in the darkened auditorium, wardens ordinarily believe that the good-will gesture is worth the risk. Besides, denial of movie privileges is an effective form of punishment. By the twentieth century, most prisons also boast of their athletic programs, so on Saturday you may be able to watch a ballgame or play on a team. You may be forced to watch a game, even if you don't want to. Once or twice a week you'll be marched to the bathhouse; and once or twice a week you'll be allowed to change your shirt and trousers. As late as 1913 Sing Sing provided one change of underclothes a week, issued damp from the wash.[15]

The laundry is a constant source of trouble. Sometimes it's used as an ugly job assignment for inmates (homosexuals, for instance) who are being punished or segregated from the rest of the population. Sometimes it's just a secluded place where favored convicts can sit around all day and run their rackets. If you "work" in a laundry like that, you can make your time worthwhile by transmitting contraband hidden in inmate uniforms.

Or you can collect bribes from inmates who actually want their clothing washed.[16] In almost every prison, the laundry is noted for its mysterious ability to lose clothing, no matter how many convict numbers were inked onto it. An inmate newspaper once gloried in the marvelous laundry at Jackson, which processed one hundred thousand items a week. Years later, the same paper revealed that the laundry made a profession of losing clothes, that weeks might be required for clothes to be returned to their wearers, and that everybody knew this was the case, but nobody did anything about it.[17] It was obvious that the staff expected bribes to do its work. Maybe the laundry had changed; more likely, it was crooked to start with.

But whatever your job assignment, you will find the working conditions peculiar. In the early days of the Big House, many American prisons claimed to turn a profit, either by selling their inmates' labor to firms that operated factories inside the walls or by running factories themselves. Since convicts were paid nothing, or next to nothing, some institutions were able to exist for a while without subsidies from the state.[18] But when one looks at the large cost of building and maintaining a prison, the paper profits dwindle. They wouldn't pay a mortgage. And the era of alleged prosperity was not to last. Labor unions and business associations waged incessant warfare against competition from prison industries. By the twentieth century, the industries were dead or dying. Those that survived made products that didn't horn in on civilian operations, usually products that were strictly for government use (office furniture, license plates, prison clothes), and they rarely made anything that could rightly be called a profit. Convict labor is slave labor, and slaves aren't needlessly energetic.

Prisons never took much heed of the suggestion, which naturally arose in a capitalist society, that convicts might learn to become normal citizens by working for profits that they could share.[19] No one was willing to pay them a substantial wage. Inmates at one state pen were fond of asking, "Why should I make bricks for Kansas?" A student of a comparatively well-run prison described what happened "so often . . . a group of five or six inmates conversing or sleeping in the corner of an industrial shop or in a storeroom, unmolested by their guard." Another able investigator of prisons estimated that inmates were idle 50 or 60 percent of the time in the not-for-profit industries of the Big House he investigated.[20] In short, if you were sentenced to serve a number of years at "hard labor," you will probably find "labor" the easiest part of your sentence.

This is bad for you, if you are one of the many convicts who came to prison without skills or education. Most prisons provide schooling for inmates who haven't finished some minimal number of grades; some also provide "vocational education." That ordinarily consists, however, of working in the prison shops, where tasks are so undemanding, and equipment is so specialized or out of date, that the education is useless. Convicts know that few civilian employers want men who are good at making license plates.[21] Prison work teaches you little more than how to be a convict.

More important in keeping you from ending up as "nothing but a con" are your contacts with family and friends—people who are always in danger of becoming former family and friends. You will have the privilege of receiving certain visitors and of writing to certain correspondents. Any letters you are allowed to write will be heavily censored (no references to crime, no references by name to any other convict, and above all, no criticism of the institution) and embarrassing as well, because you will have to write them on prison stationery, with your convict number at the top. Visits will be limited to one a week, or maybe one a month. You'll receive your visitors sitting on a stool on the far side of a five-foot table, elbow to elbow with the other cons. When your guests enter, you'll see them trying to pick you out of the crowd. You'll be acutely conscious of the number on your chest, and of the guard seated on a platform above you, watching and listening.

Some prisons allow one moment of physical contact, one hug or kiss, before convict and visitor seat themselves on opposite sides of the table. The convicts pay for that moment. It means there will be a search of their clothes and bodies, before and after the visit. And these are the best conditions you can expect. In many prisons, you will have to converse with friends and family across a wide, empty space, or through a steel-mesh barrier, or watch them through a little window while conversing by phone.

Years may pass without your touching anyone from outside the Big House.

There is some compensation. If you have any resources—tobacco, candy, money—coming to you, licitly or illicitly, from the Outside, you will find it fairly easy to purchase commodities on the Inside: drugs, liquor, young men. The first and second items are smuggled through the gates by low-paid guards; the third is generally available inside, if you can discover a safe place to enjoy it. This isn't an insuperable difficulty. In a short time, you'll find out who the dominant inmates are: the ones who work in the hospital, the chaplain's office, and the deputy warden's office; some of the "runners" and kitchen workers; and other people who have choice jobs because the administration has identified them as convict leaders. Ordinarily, "con bosses" run the prison. There aren't enough officers to supervise everything, and besides, it's easier to let the convicts operate their home industries. By slipping something to the deputy warden's clerk, you can have an attractive young inmate assigned as the second convict in your cell. But even if you don't have that kind of pull, there may be opportunities to have sex in the alley behind the kitchen, or in the factory storeroom.

If you're caught having sex, or taking food away from the mess hall, or having unauthorized articles in your cell, or making noise after lights-out, or (the all-purpose category) committing "insubordination," and if your prison has some respect for its own rules, you can expect to be disciplined. The guard who busts you may just bawl you out, or smack you with his fist or club. Or he may put you "on report," and you will have to appear in a "court" or "hearing" held by a higher-ranking officer. The court will convict you, and you will be taken off to be punished.

Punishment can take a variety of forms. If you live in a nineteenth-century prison, you may find your keepers particularly inventive in that regard. You may be locked in a dark cell and kept there on rations of bread and water. You may be forced to take down your pants so you can be paddled like a schoolboy. You may be put in a cell with your wrists chained to the bars, and your nose pointed at a solid steel outer door, eight inches away, and be left to stand there for hours at a time. ("Disgusting conditions," an official document remarked, "frequently follow this method of restraint.")[22] You may have your head locked in "the collar cap," an iron cage fastened with a padlock at the neck. You may be put in the stocks and drenched with cold water—the "shower bath" or "water cure." One of your legs may be locked to a ball and chain or an iron "Oregon boot." Your head and wrists may be locked in an iron "yoke" that will leave you writhing under its weight of thirty-five or forty pounds.[23]

If you live in a progressive prison, your punishment will be less physical. It may involve being sent to a "lower grade"—outfitted in a striped uniform and assigned to work the coal pile instead of the kitchen. Or you may simply be "deprived of privileges," such as letters and visits. At the end of the nineteenth century, about half the prisons in America officially used "physical punish-

ments."[24] From the mid-twentieth century on, officially permitted retaliation almost always consisted of deprivation of privileges; isolation, perhaps in a cell lacking normal amenities; or
loss of "good time," a standard reduction in sentence for staying
out of trouble.

When you receive your "trial" in the keepers' court, you will
lie.[25] That is what's expected of you; it's part of the play that inmates and guards are assigned to perform. Even when faced with
punishment for something you didn't do, you need to "dummy
up" and refuse to "rat" on other inmates. This is the famous
"convict code." Despite the code, you will discover that some of
your fellow prisoners are willing to inform on you, either to the
officers or to the convict bosses, so long as the informers think it
will gain them some important advantage. Because officers are
often at odds with one another, there may be competing sets of
stool pigeons, some reporting to the warden, some to his under-
lings.[26]

Everyone agrees (publicly or privately) that you can't run a
prison without informers, but the number of informers is vari-
ously estimated. A former prison superintendent suggests that
"absolutely" fewer than 5 percent of inmates inform to the administration, and his view is supported by the great majority of
inmates and former inmates who have discussed the convict
code.[27] Other experts have sometimes reached other conclusions. A veteran deputy warden at Joliet once told a new convict,
"If you figure to do something and you tell your best friend in

here, that makes three of us that know it." A Virginia inmate observed: "In twelve years I have seen more than 20,000 men come and go. Among them were a sprinkling who lived by the so called code. They saw nothing, heard nothing, knew nothing and were appreciated by the general prison population about as much as Rabbis in Berlin."[28] An Illinois inmate argued that the code was a figment of the Big House icon itself, "a huge piece of imagination used principally to give an atmosphere of romance to prisons in order that the movies may occasionally show a picture about a penitentiary and have the hero show the proper amount of 'Honor among Thieves' to make a hit with the public. . . . One half is always watching the other half for something to tell the officials." But as a prisoner, can you trust such dissenting voices? Even a "piece of imagination" can exert an influence; otherwise, why would anyone try to debunk it?[29] What makes you think it's worth the risk for you to buck the code? You ask yourself that, and you keep quiet.

You try to "do your own time," ignoring other people's problems, especially those of people who aren't a lot like you. Probably you are under the age of forty; most crimes are committed by young men. If you were older, you would understand the significance of the fact that medical care isn't in large supply in the Big House. Some institutions have in-house physicians, but the talents of doctors who would take a job in prison are likely to be limited. Prison hospitals are staffed by inmates. Until the post–

World War II era, few prisons offer anything like sufficient dental care.

Probably you are also white. If you're black, you will almost undoubtedly have a harder time in the Big House than other men. In most northern penitentiaries and reformatories, members of all races are housed in the same cellblocks and play on the same sports teams; they may also eat in the same sections of the mess hall. But if you are black, you will be assigned to the more menial jobs in the institution. Blacks wash the floor while whites do the typing and filing. Racism abounds, even among humanitarians, such as the prison reformer who could not resist captioning a picture of inmates like you in a mess hall: "Convicts about to partake of the vile grub—blacks and whites intermingled."[30]

Whatever your race, your most important concern is surviving your sentence and getting out. That's what you think about when you're lying in your bunk, one shoulder resting against the steel wall of your cell. The sounds of your fellow inmates never cease; the lights on your tier are never extinguished. And there are worse things than noise and lights.

FOUR

The Art of Humiliation

Men marching in lockstep, men dressed in stripes and wearing numbers, men stripped of their hair and staring at the prison camera that's prepared to "mug" them: these images are inseparable from the Big House. No prison movie can exist without such symbols, and realities, of deprivation and humiliation. No real prison could exist without them either.

The deepest humiliations are assaults on one's identity, and American prisons abounded in such assaults. The prison uniform was the most apparent. Its purpose was to transform men both symbolically and (to the degree that symbols establish personal identity) psychologically into convicts—convicts inside and out. The moment when a man was issued his numbered convict suit was the moment when he visibly and permanently assumed his convict role. The symbolism wasn't lost on the convicts themselves. "There is something of a shock, for a new man," writes an inmate of the modern Iowa Penitentiary, "in the prison brand stamped on his clothing of blue denim."[1] From this point on, even for him, the sight of his body will always be the sight of prison.

As disturbing as the art of humiliation could be, it had practical purposes. Prison reformers constantly bemoaned the oppressive environment of the penitentiary, its drabness and grayness; yet as a sociologist with strong reformist sentiments remarked in a classic work on prison culture, "even a fresh coat of paint in a cell may be used by an industrious prisoner to cover up his handiwork when he has cut the bars and replaced them with putty."[2] Grass and flowers can normalize a prison yard, yet the pretty landscaping can also hide a knife or a bag of drugs. Inmates benefit, in the short run, from permission to keep a supply of food, or a library of books, in their cells; but every book and every package can be used to secrete some kind of contraband or some kind of weapon that can be used on other inmates. It's easy to make the case that, for their own good, inmates in a well-run prison can be permitted only the most Spartan, literally degraded, style of life.

Humiliation can be justified—but it remains humiliation. Strip-searching an inmate after a visit with his wife is necessary to make sure she hasn't passed him any drugs; it also demonstrates to him that the institution is more important than any wife can be. Probing a new inmate's anus is necessary to keep contraband from being smuggled in; it also shows him that he no longer owns his body. Shaving an inmate's skull is helpful as prevention against lice; it also lets him know that from the institution's point of view every inmate is precisely the same as every other inmate, while being absolutely different from any normal human being. In the Robert Redford film *Brubaker* (1980) a warden begins his job by masquerading as a convict so that he can discover what convict life is like. But while dressing in, he finds it convenient to bribe the barber not to give him a real prison haircut. That would be far too real. The scene is one more indication, in case you need it, that neither wardens nor Hollywood stars actually want to become inmates, even when they're pretending to be inmates. The defining degree of humiliation is something that only real inmates suffer.

Like the head shave, the convict uniform has had several purposes, symbolic and practical, associated with its ultimate purpose of marking and transforming its wearer's identity. In prisons that have experimented with allowing inmates to wear their own clothing, they have easily been mistaken for civilians. Before a crackdown at Stateville in the 1930s, it was "almost impossible to distinguish guards from inmates." Admittedly, most prisoners can't afford to dress like civilians. They aren't wealthy enough to keep buying their own clothes—even in the twenty-first century, when clothing is cheaper than ever before. But inmates with resources will not only wear their own clothes but also create black markets in clothing, and the better-dressed inmates will reinstitute the social hierarchies of the outside world.

The aim of every prison is to create two types of beings: convicts and officers, with no status variations within the first group that can possibly cause problems for the second group. The convict uniform is like a military uniform in this respect: it is the sign of a simpler, more orderly, and more disciplined world than the one that exists outside. The dramatic "staging" of a difference between groups has been called "one of the main accomplishments of total institutions."[3]

Some prison customs, such as the head shave, depend for their effect as much on the specific context of "totality" as on anything intrinsic to the custom itself. Men entering the armed forces are routinely shaved bald. The cut may be a shock, but there is pride in enduring it. It signifies a certain kind of power: now you're a man. In the 1990s the induction cut became a status symbol among young civilians as well as young military men. The prison cut is identical, but it has usually not been experienced in the same way. As a black convict said, reflecting on his memories of the 1940s, when even a normal civilian life was by no means easy for black men, "All the jails you go in, you get a bald head. And, to me, that's the worst thing in the world can happen to you."[4]

Prison discipline was influenced in many ways by military discipline. Prison officers took military titles (sergeant, lieutenant, captain) and cultivated military customs. Yet in the case of the uniform, there was always a difference between the military world and the prison world. Nineteenth-century prison guards often wore civilian clothes; convicts almost never did. When special clothing for guards was adopted, it was frequently modeled on policemen's uniforms, for which it could sometimes be mistaken. But while a convict uniform might sometimes resemble a military one, its design was almost always distinctive enough to enforce the element of humiliation. There wasn't just a difference in context; there was an intrinsic difference.

The archetypal convict uniform—the one that is still considered appropriate for movies, cartoons, Halloween costumes, dolls, dog clothes (!), and novelty items of every kind—is a black-and-white striped coat-and-trousers combination. Generations after stripes were abolished in the vast majority of American prisons, popular journals still referred to progressive institutions as "Prison Without Stripes," thus equating stripes with the Big House in its ordinary form.[5] Few people associate the U.S. Army with uniforms from the Mexican War, or police officers with uniforms from the 1880s; but striped uniforms are permanently associated with the Big House. No other clothing style, not even the orange jumpsuit currently worn in many jails, has become interesting enough to replace prison stripes in the popular imagination.[6]

Introduced at Auburn by 1823 (and earlier at New York City's Newgate prison), the striped suit is thought to have been inspired by the arrows imprinted on the clothing of British convicts. The Auburn uniform somewhat resembled clothes worn by workmen of the time—trousers, vest, shirt, cap—except for its cheapness ($5.87 for a year's clothing, leather shoes included) and, of course, the stripes.[7] But soon the uniform evolved away from its working-class roots. In most cases, the vest was dropped, and the upper garment became a bulky tunic. A gray, collarless work shirt was often worn beneath it, but the coat was still striped, and it was no longer shaped like a normal civilian coat.

Through most of the nineteenth century, stripes were the default convict suit. Sometimes the black-and-white bars were vertical, but horizontal patterns were preferred, perhaps because some civilian clothing was vertically striped (though much less obtrusively). The usual width of the stripe was two inches. The material was wool or coarse cotton. Often a little striped "monkey cap" was added to the suit. In some prisons, especially in the South, striped trousers continued to be issued even after the upper-body uniform became a denim coat and a modern work shirt. The important thing was the symbolism, the display of the convict as a curious visual object.

The display was always popular. Cameras—whether of journalists or movie makers or postcard producers—turned automatically toward the striped uniform, especially when it was replicated in a long line of lockstepped convicts, moving across a prison yard like a giant caterpillar, or when the doors of a cellblock opened and, as a popular journal put it, the "galleries [came] alive with striped beings." Another publication, *The Youth's Companion*, America's largest-selling magazine in the early 1890s, reported that the striped convict suit turned every man who wore it into a "grotesque and gigantic insect." Moved by similar thoughts about the transformative power of clothing, humanitarians made the striped "clown suit" a major object of reform. They complained that its symbolism stole the convicts' "manhood."[8] They were right: that's what it was meant to do.

By 1920 the black-and-white-striped uniform had been abolished virtually everywhere in the North, not to return until the 1990s, and then almost exclusively in county jails and in the form of light, easy-to-use, 65 percent polyester jumpsuits and pullovers. In the intervening period, drabber forms of the convict suit prevailed. One version was a gray woolen trousers-and-coat ensemble with dark narrow pairs of horizontal stripes every few inches. Another was a parody of the military uniform, a set of "cadet gray" trousers and coat, without stripes. Accessories, in such places as Sing Sing, were a suit of underwear and a "hickory" work shirt marked with thin but still-symbolic vertical stripes, all of rough cloth, and a pair of heavy "brogan" shoes.[9] This, basically, became the stereotypical uniform in mid-twentieth-century prison movies. Stateville, Jackson, and other penitentiaries adopted parodies of civilian wear: denim coats and trousers, along with those hickory shirts. Some other prisons (Iowa, for instance) went farther and issued blue denim trousers and a plain blue work shirt—close enough to normal workwear to satisfy the reformers, but never close enough in shape or quality to make an inmate feel like a normal man.

Special uniforms might be provided for special assignments. Food servers and office workers sometimes wore white shirts on the job. But most variations were far from strictly utilitarian. In Michigan during the 1950s and 1960s, trusties working the prison farms wore baggy trousers, coats, and pullover shirts, all in brown, and all very different from the jeans and flannel shirts worn by normal civilian farmhands. Since brown was the color most likely to help a convict camouflage himself and escape from a farm, the purpose of this suit remains unknown—unless it was simply to remind the convict "trusty" that he wasn't a normal farmhand.

And that, again, is the point. Prison uniforms weren't intended to make their wearers think they were ordinary men. As one writer said of the striped suit, it had "a distinct unpleasantness and even repulsiveness of [its] own."[10] The "military" uniforms used at Elmira and other places were too plain and blocky to be taken for real military wear. The "workman's suits" used in most prisons during the twentieth century weren't real workman's clothing. There was always something different about them.

One thing was their refusal to fit. A San Quentin inmate, crawling into his coarse, heavy, badly shaped uniform, thought of himself as a "mummified creature." Whether the effect was produced by administrative choice or by administrative indifference, it wasn't accidental. Warden Lewis Lawes of Sing Sing took pride in the replacement of stripes with something closer to clothes worn on the Outside, but he was amused by the fact that most of the new convict clothing still contrived to be the wrong size for the convicts. He considered it "quite immaterial as to whether or not the clothes fit, and they usually do not. The result is that when dressed the prisoner would scarcely be recognized by anyone except his most intimate acquaintances."[11]

The social importance of clothes that don't fit is emphasized by *20,000 Years in Sing Sing* (1932), a movie reputedly based on Lawes's experience. The actor impersonating "Warden Long" (Arthur Byron) declares that "people on the outside are supposed to be created free and equal, but they aren't. In here, they really are. One inmate is just as good as another inmate." Immediately after this exposition of political theory, we see the warden's ideas in action, as new inmates are forced to don their numbered uniforms, whether they fit or not. These men may not be as free as people outside the walls, but they are, indeed, a lot more equal— and a lot more humiliated. An inmate in Illinois said, "Why all clothes are issued three or four sizes too large I have never been able to fathom."[12] Lawes, and "Long," provide an explanation.

Another sign of the convict's difference from the civilian is the number stenciled on his suit. For ordinary purposes of identification, numbers are less practical than names: they're harder to remember, and ultimately they have to be matched to names anyway. But as an insult to personal identity, a convict number works very well. It may appear in a variety of locations: in one-inch digits on the shirttail and the inside of the trousers, as in Iowa in the 1950s; in two-inch digits across the back of the shirt, as at Stateville from the 1930s through the 1950s; or in modest half-inch figures on a white label affixed to the convict's chest and rump, as in innumerable prisons of the present time. The essential thing is the transformation of personal identity into institutional identity—a process so potent that many reformers regarded the abolition of visible numbers as a crucial step in transforming the Big House itself.

When Clinton Duffy became warden of San Quentin in 1940, one of his first orders was the elimination of the "big numbers stamped in black on every inmate's clothes." "We rob a man of his identity," he lamented; "we rub out his name and give him a number instead." So strongly did he feel about this issue that, pending the arrival of new uniforms, he had the numbers on the old ones painted out with India ink. According to Duffy, some inmates attached even more importance to their numbers than he did: they hated them, but when they got out of prison they had difficulty living without them.[13]

However that may be, the convict number and the convict uniform were indispensable to the Big House. Duffy wished he "could do away with numbers entirely," but he couldn't, and neither can the prisons of the twenty-first century.[14] Gone are the days when, it is claimed, inmates were "never referred to by name," only by number.[15] But although the numbers have sometimes retreated from the outside of the inmate's clothing to his "jacket" in the records file, they are always ready to reemerge, whether on the clothing itself or on a big plastic badge, clipped to a prominent place on his anatomy. Convict numbers and convict uniforms have always gone together, and neither is prepared to go away.

In the 1970s and 1980s, when the idea of the Big House was in disrepute, and radical reforms were occurring in prisons throughout the country, some state penitentiaries tried to lessen the difference between Inside and Outside by permitting inmates to wear civilian clothes. In Washington State biker gangs flaunted their "colors"; in Michigan convicts sported the same "pimp" costumes they had worn on the streets of Detroit. Old-time prison workers regarded all this as the last stage of institutional demoralization—and that was true, on custodial as well as aesthetic grounds. When convicts wear their own clothing, they look like civilians, and they tend to act like them. Reformers and traditionalists agreed on that. The question was, Do you want them to act that way? The answer was a resounding No.

The Big House never regained its aesthetic purity, but some of its traditions proved more resilient than reformists had anticipated. Nowhere was there a more vigorous reaction in support of tradition than in the campaign to make inmates look like inmates. The officers' union at Stateville—itself a product of the new thinking about prisons—started the trend in 1971 by urgently demanding "a set of rules for dress and grooming for inmates and Officers alike."[16] By the end of the 1990s, both uniforms and definite regulations governing their use had returned almost everywhere in the country, and the more obviously "convict" a uniform appeared, the more likely it was to be required. Stripes and bright orange jumpsuits (a new contribution to the aesthetics of humiliation) proliferated in jails and transport vans.

Distinctively shaped and colored work sets were favored by penitentiaries—modern successors of traditional Big House costumes, designed not just to clothe people but also to make them unmistakably into convicts. Once again, numbers were unapologetically annexed to chests. As a concession to progressive sentiments, the convict's last name was usually added to his number; but to compensate, jails and prisons frequently stenciled "INMATE" in huge letters across their prisoners' backs.

In Michigan an epic battle was fought over numbers and uniforms. Civil-liberties lawsuits delayed enforcement of uniform codes from 1988 to 1998, when a monumentally determined Department of Corrections finally regained the ability to tell its prisoners what to wear. The DOC's aesthetic statement was a dark blue cotton-polyester shirt-and-trouser combination, vaguely reminiscent of a civilian work set, but with orange stripes running down each leg and across each shoulder. It was the right touch: conservative, decorous, not at all triumphant about the DOC's victory over the reformist meddlers, yet definite in announcing: "*This* is a convict." The ultimate artistic expression came in 2001, when all convict uniforms were stamped with two-inch numbers across the back and down the leg.[17] Now there could be no question about what belonged to whom, or who belonged to what.

The popular media had never stopped equating convicts with numbers and uniforms, striped or unstriped. *Life* defined prisoners as "Men with Numbers"; MGM saw prison itself as a *House of*

Numbers, its title for a film about the subject (1957).[18] *Coronet*, the poor man's *Life*, took a similar approach, dramatizing the moment when a convict gets his number as his crucial moment of transformation. In a *Coronet* picture story we see a fresh-faced young man, the image of vulnerability, sitting on a prison bench, looking up at a burly guard. The caption reads: "To the receiving officer, all prisoners are names who must be given numbers"—an invitation to see the convict from the officer's perspective, as an object to be labeled.[19]

In the defining scene of the movie *Convicts Four* (1962), the camera emphasizes the distinction between control and servitude by dwelling on the contrast between the warden (Broderick Crawford), a fat man in a sloppy business suit, lounging in a thronelike chair, and the new fish (Ben Gazzara), a slender young man standing nervously before him, lost in the crude convict coat he keeps buttoned up to his neck (he has been told, "You will at all times be lined up, buttoned up, and shut up"). There is clearly a difference, as one of the numbered convicts in *The Shawshank Redemption* (1994) says, between a convict and a real person, a person who "can wear a suit and a tie." That's also the idea in *20,000 Years in Sing Sing*, in which Tommy Connors (Spencer Tracy), a famous gangster, is told that the "castle on the Hudson" to which he's just been sentenced will be "quite a change: . . . no tailor shop." Lacking tailored clothes, Connors will soon be "just a number."

The movie gloats over the new inmate's humiliation. But whether the effect is gloating or compassion or a number of emotions that aren't so easy to specify, the idea of having a number, of being a number, has a curious appeal for Americans, people who are otherwise noted for the value they place on "being yourself." Part of the explanation may lie precisely in the fact that Americans view personal identity as the shrine of all good things. Violate personal identity, and you are sure to elicit strong and interesting feelings. Pity for another person's humiliation, admiration for his resistance to repression, satisfaction about the punishment he may deserve for his own bad choices, relief that none of this is happening to *you* ("Haveing an awfull tireing [*sic*] week," someone writes on the back of a Jackson Prison postcard; but "what if one had to be shut up in here[?]")[20]—the feelings evoked by institutional assaults on identity can take many forms, but they are certain to be vivid.

The aesthetic appeal of "men with numbers" may also result from the fact that what is important in a movie or other work of art isn't the simple representation of reality (few people actually want to pay for that); it's the transformation of reality. The art of the Big House itself was emphatically the art of transformation, both on the grand scale of the walls and towers of an artificial world and on the small scale of ordinary men locked into that world and transformed into convicts. This was the institutional program of the Big House; this was the heart of its peculiar aesthetic, and this was the interesting thing it offered to movies, television, and magazines.

So closely associated with the idea of prison is the idea of transformation that rituals of transformation are considered obligatory in prison stories, even when they compete with the stories' ostensible themes. *Prison* (1988—an early showpiece for Viggo Mortensen) is a horror movie in which a ghost haunts an old Big House—the former Wyoming State Penitentiary (1901–81), playing itself. A large proportion of this film is spent simply surveying the architecture of the prison and showing new inmates dressing in. Prison dramas that don't have to compete with the need for horror can do even more with these concepts.

Shawshank, one of the most popular of America's many hundreds of prison films, uses transformation as its theme and the prison uniform as its salient image.[21] The protagonist is a young banker who is sent to the Big House for a crime he didn't commit. When he arrives, his identity is immediately overwhelmed by the uniform he is forced to wear: ill-fitting denim trousers and a gray striped shirt stamped with a big convict number on the left chest: 37927. The transformation is emphasized by his job assignment—slopping dirty uniforms in the laundry. He is now an inmate like other inmates, degraded, undifferentiated except by number, lost in a swamp of disgusting materiality. When at last he succeeds in breaking out of the Big House, the act is pictured as an escape from the all-enveloping uniform. As soon as he reaches the Outside, he strips off his numbered shirt and lets the free rain cleanse his naked skin. Practically "all they found of him," we are told, "was a muddy set of prison clothes"—the remains of his convict identity.

But this man's escape, the film assures us, is the exception that proves the rule. For almost everyone else, the uniform is something you can't remove. Like the Big House, it's impossible to get out of. In the movie's second-most-dramatic scene, a personable young convict is shot down by order of the warden. The execution is presented as a series of transformations taking place within the convict's numbered shirt. At the start, the uniform is clean and neat, a sign of his own sincerity and vulnerability. At the end, it's a target, full of bloody holes. The uniform, the summation of convict identity, has claimed another victim.

That's the verdict in *Shawshank:* few men escape the numbered suit. But the convict uniform is so potent a symbol of transformation that by the end of the twentieth century it had transformed itself into a medium of the counterculture—or of currents in popular culture that could not be identified except by projection onto their antithesis, the Big House. The uniform that was intended to annihilate assertive masculinity became an image of masculinity itself.

In *Jailhouse Rock* (1957), the most memorable in the long series of movies that exploited Elvis Presley's sexuality, Elvis plays a naive young man who is sent to prison for killing someone in a bar fight. The crime has no meaning, but the punishment has a considerable amount of sex appeal. The jailhouse episodes of the movie are full of fetishes of masculinity, the special kind of masculinity that shows itself in conditions in which masculinity is officially denied. Elvis's prison uniform is the primary fetish. It's nothing special, just a fairly typical mid-twentieth-century jeans-and-work-shirt combination, with a big set of numbers on the left chest of the coat: 6239, stenciled in black, one inch tall. Yet the camera loves that coat, especially when it's loosely draped over Elvis's naked androgynous torso, after he's been strung up and whipped as punishment for a prison misdemeanor (socking a guard). Whipping wasn't customary in Big Houses in 1957, but it was still in vogue in Hollywood. Unlike the painfully well-tailored uniforms that asserted Elvis's masculinity in the publicity stills about his army service, the prison suit, with its bulk and intransigence and total lack of fashion, allows him to exhibit toughness as well as vulnerability. The convict is as resistant as the coat. That's a lot to get into a third-rate film.

In the movie's big musical number—the only sequence that anyone remembers—Elvis and a crowd of male dancers perform the title song, a celebration of a mythical lockup where the convicts spend their time dancing with one another and saying things like "you're the cutest jailbird I ever did see." This is a prison where you can "get [your] kicks," where being locked up is something gay, in both senses of the word—one of them unintentional, perhaps, but real and evident. The costumes reinforce the impression that this triumph of male vitality can happen only in a separate world, where men are supposed to be degraded, but somehow aren't. Elvis's nondescript prison work shirt is replaced by a garment even more strongly associated with humiliation, a shirt with broad black and white convict stripes—

a suggestion that the strongest sexual allure comes from the strongest symbols of degradation. There's still a big number on his chest, but now it's 6240, as if the convict were making progress, if only by one digit.

The connection between prison life and maleness, degraded yet triumphant, became an influence on civilian fashion in the 1990s, when baggy, droopy, badly fitted convict denims became a style statement for young men on the Outside. The "sagger" look spread quickly from the inner city, where ex-convicts are numerous, to the prosperous suburbs, and it hasn't completely gone away. As a symbol of masculinity, a masculinity strong enough to vindicate itself against the pressures of regimentation (whether in prison or, less convincingly, an expensive private school), it illustrates the capacity of Big House images to transform themselves, evolving new kinds of significance. In the 1930s convicts wanted trousers that were "reasonably tight in the buttock," like the tailored trousers that civilians wore.[22] The loose, shambling convict costume was a sign of shame. Now civilians were seeing it as a reward for valor.

Every icon has an inside and an outside. The inside is the facts, the basic reality. The outside is all the facets of that reality in which observers identify reflections of themselves—reflections that dramatize or distort the observers' own reality, or reveal their fears and fantasies. The subject of the next chapter is sexual fantasies and realities.

FIVE

Sex

Picture yourself in the serving line of a prison mess hall. Suddenly a beefy, fortyish convict comes through the door, accosts a pretty young man, picks him up, and carries him off, screaming. No one objects or even pays much attention to what is evidently a common occurrence.

A rape scene like that is highly unlikely to happen in any real prison, however rough. But it happens, and is even made to seem remotely plausible, in *Brubaker*, an attempted exposé of life as it is really lived in American prisons.

For current popular culture, a defining feature of prison is homosexuality, and especially homosexual violence. In films of the past three decades, rape is a standard part of virtually any prison setting, no matter what distortions of reality are necessary to get it into the plot. If movies have any influence on reality, it is possible that this incorporation of rape into the prison icon has promoted the acceptance of sexual violence, by both convicts and civilians, as if it were a mere fact of life.[1] The advertising poster for the recent film *Let's Go to Prison* (2006) shows a single image: a bar of soap, engraved with the movie's title, lying next to a shower drain. Two things are interesting about this image: first, everyone is expected to know what it means (men constantly get raped in prison showers, so "don't drop the soap"); second, everyone is expected to laugh. *Let's Go to Prison* is supposed to be a comedy.

Many Americans find it easy to believe that the images I've just mentioned are faithful and sufficient representations of reality. They aren't. Yet describing the reality of prison sex is very difficult.

How common was sex in the Big House? If one believes the pop-Freudian idea that "sexual energy" cannot be successfully repressed but will always reassert itself, then it follows that every convict's sex drive is bound to find an "outlet" and that every prison will be full of homosexual relationships. Prison camps in the South sometimes allowed male inmates to have sex with women during what are now called "conjugal visits," but the practice was rare in other American penal institutions, except when a corrupt regime made it possible for bribery to purchase anything the convicts wanted. (It is still rare.) The Big House was the enemy of heterosexual desire; so if the "outlet" theory is true, it was a separate world in large part because it was a pervasively homosexual world.

But is the theory true? Even for today's prisons, statistics about sexual behavior vary to an almost ludicrous extent. This is not surprising; they are generally based on self-reports of convicts or officers who for their own reasons agree to respond to surveys, surveys conducted in a variety of ways and with widely varying degrees of objectivity.[2] Accounts by well-informed writers differ greatly, even from themselves. In the 1950s an otherwise responsible journalist concluded, simultaneously, that there were "only a few . . . true homosexuals" in prison and that a majority of men "no doubt" have sex in "long-term" prisons. Despite the paucity of "true homosexuals," he opined, prison homosexuality may be "all but universal"; all prisons are enveloped by "a homosexual miasma," constituting "the most difficult problem a warden faces."[3]

Standing on one side of this debate is a warden of long experience who doubts that prison life makes men homosexual and observes that few, if any, sexual "predators" had not been predators before they came to prison. An inmate writer finds himself on another side: "Salt thirteen hundred men away where they can't get to women and some of them are going to find substitutes. . . . Depriving prisoners of sex life is the greatest part of prison punishment, and it has also made hopeless perverts of thousands of men with thousands of years to spend in a womanless world."[4] The administration at Stateville tried to have it both ways. It assured new inmates that they would never "be tempted to practice sex perversion" unless there was "something fundamentally wrong" with them; it also cautioned these presumably normal men against being misled by "smutty stories," "indecent suggestions," and simple "curiosity"—as if homosexuality weren't so hard to catch, after all. A sociologist employed at Stateville from 1957 to 1963 recalled that "voluntary homosexual activity was pervasive (though by no means rampant)"; he had heard of only one rape—a fact he attributed to the prison's tight management.[5]

One would like to have enough facts, and be certain enough of them, to make general statements about sex in prison. Unfortunately, sufficient and conclusive evidence is hard to find, and one's view of particular kinds of evidence is influenced by what one accepts as plausible answers to basic questions about sex itself.

There is, to start with, the question of how widespread homosexuality is in the world *outside* the walls. It is hard enough to answer this question with regard to the sex-affirming, obsessively self-surveying twenty-first century, let alone with regard to the nineteenth century, when you could be sent to prison for homosexual conduct.[6] Another question is how to define homosexuality. Is it "really homosexuality" when a self-proclaimed "straight" convict has sex with an effeminate male whom he says he regards as a "girl," or when male rape is used to assert racial or other forms of dominance? Most writers on the subject answer No— although the difficulty of altering habits of sexual arousal argues Yes, and the impossibility of knowing what images occupy the minds of males who are having sex with other captive males, some of whom they call "girls," "punks," and "bitches," suggests no more than Maybe.[7] Are heterosexuality and homosexuality (or, for that matter, bisexuality) inherent and essentially unchangeable, or are they shaped importantly by circumstance? Depending on one's answer to that question, which has philosophical and personal, as well as statistical, dimensions, one will tend either to embrace or to ignore various kinds of statistical surveys and official reports on prison sex.

Much of our information about sex in the Big House period comes from summary comments, representing a wide range of impressions, though tending toward the lurid. A 1925 report from the Missouri State Penitentiary maintained, "Few of the young boys [who] came in here . . . did not soon succumb to this." At Sing Sing, according to the report of a 1913 grand jury investigation, men were having sex in the shower room and cells; "sodomy is rife." In appalled tones the investigators announced, "We find negroes and whites have shared the same cells."[8] This complaint, which was entered next to the discussion of "sexual perversion," registered the fear that blacks and whites were going so far as to have sex with one another.

That issue aside, everyone considered it unwise (though often necessary) to house two inmates in a cell—so unwise that in 1898 the Kansas Industrial Reformatory paroled inmates in order to prevent double-celling and the accompanying "detestable practices." In New York it was viewed as "unscientific" to house convicts in dormitories, where "immorality abounds," or to let them crowd together in the shower room. In 1957 *Life* accused old-time "prisonkeepers" of "naiveté" about homosexuality, then displayed its own naiveté by telling readers that the problem was now being solved by one-man cells, the segregation of "obvious homosexuals," and "well-supervised dormitor[ies]." The old-timers weren't that naive, although they sometimes had quaint ways of talking about sex. The warden who came to Sing Sing in 1914 likened the prison's problem of "immorality" to similar problems in the navy. He wrote of "ordinary men placed under unnatural conditions," men who could benefit (in his mild phrasing) from more exercise in "self-control."[9]

In neither published nor unpublished sources from the Big House period does one find consensus about the customary punishment for sexual relations. One informed opinion is that "frequently" both participants in a sex act were punished, and sometimes "the punishment [was] very severe." From the same period—indeed, from the same author—comes the report that "whenever possible" guards who found prisoners in a compromising situation let them escape with a warning.[10] Other testimony both supports and opposes the idea that little was done to prevent prison sex. Warden John Kennedy of Sing Sing found himself in serious legal trouble because the grand jury concluded, among other things, that he made "no effort" to prevent homosexual cell assignments and that "acts of sexual perversion are taken for granted." But the grand jury didn't take them for granted.[11]

When prison wardens took resolute action against homosexuality, it usually consisted simply of segregating "known homosexuals." At Elmira in the 1930s, "sex perverts" were housed in the prison's Psychopathic Clinic, together with "others who [were] potentially psychotic." The total population of the clinic, however, was only about 3 or 4 percent of the institution, implying that few inmates who had homosexual relations were regarded as dangerously "perverted."[12] Warden Ragen of Stateville put gay men in single cells and posted yellow cards over the doors—until, he said with a sneer, he found that the men "liked the advertising." Warden Duffy of San Quentin created a special cellblock for "known aggressive homosexuals" (around 2 percent of the population). These "unfortunate individuals" were made to work together in the laundry "under special guard." Duffy claimed that segregation of homosexuals reduced violence by 90 percent, because more fights were generated by sex and romance than by anything else.[13]

Before 1948, when Alfred Kinsey's report on *Sexual Behavior in the Human Male* suggested that homosexuality was much more common, either in prison or out of it, than anybody had guessed, few books or articles about prisons focused on the sex problem.[14] Nevertheless, those that mentioned "perversion" tended to regard it as a constant feature of imprisonment, a *normal* feature, if you will.[15] They made various estimates of its frequency, but they saw it as a regular, though ugly, part of the landscape. Their attitude opens an interesting vista on American society during what is often regarded as a more innocent, or more ignorant, age than our own. Long before homosexuality became a common topic of conversation in America, many supposedly unsophisticated citizens of little prison towns must have had considerable knowledge of the subject.[16]

Odd pieces of the puzzle turn up. A long letter written in 1937 by a convict to the warden of Maine's state prison shows that this official routinely warned prisoners with histories of homosexuality to stay away from younger inmates, whose sexual favors might be sold for "as high as $5" ($75 in today's money). "This is a tough place," the inmate says, "for a young man or boy who is over passionate and [has] no means to appease his passions except with his hand. . . . Boys . . . are subjected to unusual temptations, temptations that too many boys yield to to get the money with which to buy luxuries or to gamble."[17]

That's one bit of information. Another is the fact that more than half the words about sex in the sex-filled argot of the Big House referred to homosexuality.[18] Yet another is a claim that in the 1920s the San Quentin band performed every Sunday for the Jocker's Ball, an event in which "hundreds of jockers [aggressive, 'masculine' homosexuals] and queens ['feminine' homosexuals] waltzed and fox-trotted under the 300-foot-long iron roof in the Big Yard."[19] If these parties took place, they were evidence of how successful inmates could be in creating their own customs and making the Big House into their own form of art. And if they took place, they were certainly known and understood by many people outside the walls, whose thoughts on the issue have been lost to history.

Not so the thoughts of Alexander Berkman, a "communist anarchist" who in 1892 tried to assassinate Henry Clay Frick, a leading executive in the steel industry, and in payment spent many years in the Western Penitentiary of Pennsylvania. Berkman's memoirs describe a number of prison love affairs. A product of Victorian romanticism, he depicts them not just as predictable results of sex deprivation but also as sentimental friendships: "He reminded me of a girl I used to court. . . . He put both hands between the bars, and pressed his lips to mine." But lurking behind the ideal friendships are the more common affairs of "'the girls,' 'Sallies,' and 'punks,' who for gain traffic in sexual gratification." There are also customs that Berkman assumes are universal in reformatories. "De older boys in de ref," a young convict tells him, "always used me, an' dey use all de kids. But dey was no friends."[20]

In 1933 a convict memoir called *Prison Days and Nights* frankly and extensively described homosexual customs in prison. It said, for instance, that the Naval Prison at Portsmouth "was an absolute bawdy house."[21] But the first book published specifically about the subject appears to have been *Sex in Prison* (1934), by Joseph Fishman, a lawyer who served as federal inspector of prisons. Fishman's publisher expressed surprise that the problem of homosexuality, though formidable, was rarely explored by penological experts: "The voluminous literature concerning American prisons is not only sparse when it comes to deal with this important subject of sex, but has evaded its discussion as much as possible. The prison officials with whom the publisher communicated were wary and non-committal. The social workers with whom he spoke, usually so logical and articulate, could give him little additional information." The executive secretary of the Pennsylvania Prison Society was happy to tell Fishman's publisher that in the ninety years of the Society's *Journal*, "any discussion of sex problems in prisons, has been successfully avoided."[22]

Fishman had a tough row to hoe. Most of his opinions, however, were merely those of the psychological experts of his time. He coupled homosexuality with masturbation, "this horrible practice," and regarded it as a "perversion," albeit a perversion that was, in a sense, quite natural: all people have homosexual tendencies, and these are bound to be excited by the conditions of life in captivity. His solution, or palliative, was also less than surprising: single cells, segregation of inveterate homosexuals, and plenty of work and sports, to burn off the convicts' sexual energy.[23]

More colorful is his impression of what happens when the sex practices of the Big House are left to take care of themselves. This appears in an account, which he presents as typical, of a pretty young fish and his first days in prison. "When we went into the yard on Saturday afternoon," the convict recalls, "several men came up to me and spoke to me and two of them got into a fight. The guards came running up and separated them. I didn't know what they were fighting about and several prisoners standing around watching the fight just laughed when I asked them about it. I know now that they were fighting over me. The guards chased all the prisoners away and one of them said to me 'Watch out kid, one of those buzzards will get you.' I didn't know what he meant." The boy insisted that before coming to prison he had sexual fantasies about girls, but after he was inside for a while, they became fantasies about men—another testimony to the transformative power of the Big House.[24]

Fishman's work wasn't followed up in any systematic way. One successor who tried to be systematic was Donald Clemmer, a sociologist who attempted an exhaustive analysis of life in the Southern Illinois Penitentiary. Clemmer's influential book contains a chapter about sex, in which he speculates that 30 percent of convicts veer into "abnormal" sexuality, while another 10 percent are "abnormal" to begin with. He argues, however, that the 30 percent are thinking of women while having sex with men—or while masturbating, since he considers masturbation abnormal among free adults. ("Excessive" masturbation leads to "disintegration of the personality.") The fact that he puts "the habitual masturbator" in this "quasi-abnormal" category does little to create trust in his statistics. He admits, in addition, that his data were derived from consultation with only a small number of convicts and officers. Clemmer's theoretical framework was naively Freudian, full of unsupported claims about "regression," "fixation," and so forth, and much that makes for entertaining reading today.[25]

But Clemmer's sexology was the height of common sense,

compared with the views proffered by "scientific" reports that addressed the problems of homosexuality and masturbation in prison. High-class physicians asked themselves whether it might be a good idea to "asexualize, or sterilize against his will, a sexually morbid prisoner." Some regretfully noted that severing nerves and blistering the anus and penis didn't "offer much encourage-ment" for the "cure" of homosexuality, which, they said, was a "mental disease," although its "basic cause" was "frustration." They left the reader to reconcile such apparent contradictions. Scholarly emphasis on sexual "morbidity" persisted throughout the Big House period, a survival of the attitude toward crime that was popularized by the penological "science" of Zebulon Brockway and other nineteenth-century corrections experts— the idea that divergence from the moral norm is symptomatic of a morbid condition of the mind or body. A publicity brochure about the Indiana Reformatory, published about 1909, informs the reader that "crime is a disease. . . . The trouble lies deep down in the breast of society and the required treatment is that which gets right down to the root of the thing and kills it out."[26] What all that meant is hard to say; but homosexuality was clearly very hard to "kill out."

Regardless of the dearth of substantial literature on the sub-ject, homosexuality in prison wasn't exactly hidden from the pub-lic eye. The Love That Dare Not Speak Its Name announced it-self rather frequently, and sometimes flamboyantly. One dramatic revelation occurred in 1893–94, when Brockway's management of Elmira Reformatory was investigated by state officials and muckraking journalists, enraged about his use of corporal punishment. Their inquiries directed attention to "unmentionable vices" at Elmira, particularly those uncovered by Brockway himself in "the January deal," his attempt to extirpate homosexual behavior in the prison's pipe shop. As he testified, "there was a great deal of it in the place." He found sixty-four young men guilty of the crime, about one convict out of twenty-two in the reformatory. Even in that era, no effort was made to deny the frequency of sex in prison. Brockway labeled homosexuality a "corruption of character prevalent with prisoners," and went so far as to comment on the problems of his own youth, when, as he suggested, he might have become a criminal or a sodomite but had been rescued by circumstance, and by a psychological shock treatment administered by his father.[27]

An even bigger story was the 1915 prosecution of Warden Thomas Mott Osborne of Sing Sing for allegedly having enjoyed romantic relationships with the young inmates under his charge. Osborne beat the rap (see chapter 8); but the case showed how easy it was for people to picture the world behind the walls as a realm of exotic pleasures as well as harsh restraints and punishments.[28]

A particularly vivid image of that world was presented by the great riot at Jackson Prison in 1952. Even before this event, officers were concerned that too many sex criminals were being sent to Jackson, and that the administration itself was going gay.

A civilian counselor was caught having sex with a convict, and prison guards drew the (false) conclusion "that all the counselors were punks."[29] The riot began when Ray Young, a handsome, twenty-four-year-old homosexual inmate, tricked a neophyte guard into opening his cell in the segregation block. Young took the guard's keys and started liberating other inmates. Orgies immediately began. A gay convict had sex with fourteen men, first willingly, then unwillingly. They "formed a line at his cell door." Other men paired off to make love in private. As the riot spread to the rest of the institution, horrified reporters watched a young man being chased down and raped. When, ten years later, some newsreel footage from the riot was used in a prison movie, the voice-over referred to episodes that were omitted—"scenes that though recorded on film cannot be shown to a public audience." In the words of a prison official who was not entirely in control of his tone, "it was just a big picnic. . . . Homosexual acts were going on in broad view for anyone to see, meat was being roasted, games of chance had started . . . " When it was time for the rioters to come to terms with authorities, the convict negotiator proposed to delay surrender because "some of the inmates wanted another night with the homosexuals." At riot's end, twenty-three inmates were charged with various offenses, nine of them with sodomy; and the warden condemned the state for having sent teenage convicts into a "cesspool of depravity."[30]

Thirteen years before, Jackson had been the site of some Inside press coverage of homosexuality. Jackson's nationally distributed inmate newspaper published a rare, perhaps unique, public debate about sex as inmates saw it. A convict who preferred to be anonymous started things off by arguing that prisons could not "rehabilitate" men for normal life, because prison life was predicated on the frustration of normal sex drives. He believed that "the percentage of those who actually go off the deep end of sex is very small," but that all prisoners are "contaminated by the un-natural atmosphere." His comments were attacked by other inmates, who maintained that temptations could be resisted. Yet one of the instigator's most important questions remained unanswered: "I wonder if any of our governmental heads have ever seen a per capita degeneracy statement."[31] Perhaps his question didn't need an answer. Obviously, none of them had. Conclusive statistics about "degeneracy" didn't exist. They don't exist today.

At the time of the debate, the warden at Jackson was Joel Moore, a former college professor. He wore wire-rimmed glasses and was known as a "Modern Penologist." He recognized that "degeneracy" was a significant problem and made sure to lecture new inmates about "the cunning practices of the sex deviates." The effect of his lectures is not recorded. Fourteen years later, after the big riot, an official report said that the prison's "atmosphere" was "permeated to an unusual degree with the foul vapors of sex perversion, nauseating to the majority of the prisoners, who detest perversion and the pervert, but deadly to those who lack the strength or the inclination to resist the slow poison in the air."[32] This statement, though emphatic, was completely use-less, either as analysis or as exhortation.

It's a long way from florid condemnations of homosexuality to the comedy of *Let's Go to Prison*. The two are separated by a half-century in the evolution of American attitudes, a half-century during which popular views of sex and violence became steadily more "liberal," or perhaps more superficial, and popular views of prison recurred, eventually, to a condition as "conservative," or perhaps as cynical, as the one that existed at the start. After a heady romance with prison reform in the 1960s and 1970s, Americans began, once again, to question whether the welfare of prisoners was worth worrying about. At the same time, American culture had come to operate on the principle that no thoughts about sex are too coarse for public enjoyment, at least in an "adult" context. Hence the ease with which both liberal and con-servative talk shows and blogs now retail fantasies of revenge on political enemies, picturing distinguished members of the op-position being sent to prison, put in striped uniforms, and raped by other convicts. Hence the constant TV, movie, and Internet jokes about dropping soap in a prison shower.

We will witness the convergence of "liberal" and "conserva-tive" attitudes again. Yet the concept of prison as a place where men are deprived of their maleness has appeared in academic lit-erature for many years. "A society composed exclusively of men," says the author of a work published in 1958, "tends to generate anxieties in its members concerning their masculinity regardless of whether or not they are coerced, bribed, or seduced into an overt homosexual liaison."[33] Anxieties about masculinity are hardly limited to prisons, but for popular American culture, prison is a perfect vehicle for expressing these anxieties and using them as sources of comedy and sexual titillation, as well as inspirations for "social thought."

It's another example of the *Jailhouse Rock* phenomenon—the sexualization of prison, the use of the Big House as a screen for the projection of sexual conflicts and fantasies. I say "Big House" advisedly: the setting of these fantasies is seldom some low-security prison dorm; it's a fully equipped, old-fashioned penitentiary. Here fantasies both of sexual humiliation and of sexual dominance and fulfillment can be cultivated, all licensed by the accepted public image of the Big House. Prison sex has become a major theme of both heterosexual and homosexual pornography. Both kinds of porn exploit leading features of the Big House icon: "hard time," "men in cages" (or women in manlike cages), numbers, uniforms, overbearing guards, initiation scenes, the enforced transformation of identity.[34] The power of the icon is suggested by the fact that these features are often registered only by "peripheral" signals. The prison that the viewer actually sees in a pornographic video may be nothing more than a barred window or a piece of striped clothing, but the single image is charged with enough iconic force to bring the drama of the Big House into full erotic life.

This doesn't preclude more elaborate presentations of prison as an erotic world. *Oz* (1997–2003), the popular cable television series, is a complex re-creation of the life of an imaginary Big House. Some accommodations are made to the passage of time. The prison in *Oz* is brutally contemporary in its physical design; the staff, like that of many late-twentieth-century prisons, shows an absurd inability to control the inmates; and the whole production often looks like a satire of American prisons of the 1970s and 1980s, when discipline evaporated and the convicts "took over." The series moralizes about the evils of prison as an institution, although the megaviolence of the inmates renders this moralism somewhat beside the point.[35] Prison reform is not the emphasis or, undoubtedly, the goal of *Oz*. The goal is to realize the Big House aesthetic, to create a self-sufficient, purposely unnatural world, a total environment in which men are initiated, humiliated, and transformed in interesting ways—especially, in this case, sexually. In such an environment, the audience is encouraged to believe, one can experience all the possibilities of erotic life, so long as they are violent and cruel. *Oz* is one example of fantasy run wild. Others are readily available: Internet groups and story and picture sites in which every detail of incarceration is explored for erotic purposes, sometimes by people who aim at close replication of the Big House environment.

This kind of erotica is an aspect of American culture that has had no difficulty going global. The worldwide Internet market for prison uniforms, new or used prison cells and equipment, "old-time" cuffs and shackles, and other penal paraphernalia shows that the romantic appeal of the Big House is international, and that American concepts are still the industry standard. No one on the Internet appears to believe that prisons in Germany or France or Japan have anything to rival the historical American prison in its appeal to the sexual imagination.

In its day, the Big House was praised as an agent of moral reform and denounced as a destroyer of normal sexuality. It's not certain how well it performed in either role. But in the realm of fantasy, the Big House became potent indeed. Few institutions evoke sexual fetishes and preoccupations, or surround themselves with sexual mystery and allure.[36] The Big House did, and does.

Fig. 1. The basic box: Sing Sing in the early twentieth century
(Author's collection)

Fig. 2. The Big House as a palace in a fairy tale: Michigan's reformatory
at Ionia (Author's collection)

Fig. 3. Versailles on the pond:
the reformatory at Mansfield, Ohio (Author's collection)

Fig. 4. The perfection of architecture at
the Iowa state reformatory (Author's collection)

Fig. 5. Railroaded to prison (Author's collection)

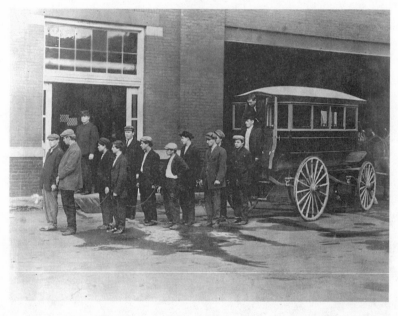

Fig. 6. The fish line: Elmira Reformatory
(Courtesy Chemung County Historical Society, Elmira, New York)

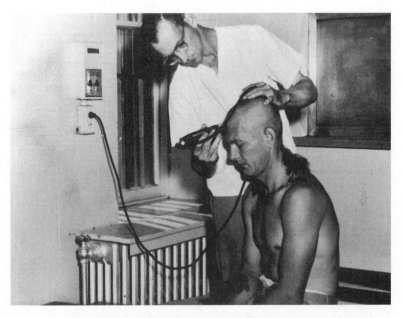

Fig. 7. Haircut (Courtesy Joliet Area Historical Museum, Joliet, Illinois)

Fig. 8. September 30, 1906: a day of transformation at the Washington
State Penitentiary. J. T. Bishop, age seventeen, shoemaker,
ten years for grand larceny (Author's collection)

Fig. 9. Convicts receiving the benefits of medical science (Author's collection)

Fig. 10. The human caterpillar: intimacy enforced at Joliet
(Courtesy Abraham Lincoln Presidential Library)

Fig. 11. The comedy of men in stripes: postcard, 1908 (Author's collection)

Fig. 12. The sequel to lockstep and stripes (Author's collection)

Fig. 13. Convicts at Stateville watching the inking of their numbers.
Fish wear temporary fatigues; officers wear smiles.
(Courtesy Illinois Department of Corrections)

Fig. 14. When inmate products made a "profit"
(Courtesy Joliet Area Historical Museum, Joliet, Illinois)

Fig. 15. Not-so-hard labor in an Illinois pen
(Courtesy Abraham Lincoln Presidential Library)

Fig. 16. Ethnic equality in the Kansas state reformatory (Author's collection)

Fig. 17. Zebulon Brockway reviewing his toy soldiers
(Courtesy Chemung County Historical Society, Elmira, New York)

Manacled to their Cell-Door Day after Day.

Fig. 18. The inmate as victim and hero: Elmira's
disciplinary practices, as represented by
the *New York World*, 1894

Fig. 19. Friendship can also exist:
buddies in an Illinois prison, 1950s (Author's collection)

Fig. 20. Joseph Ragen on the largest stage in America: mess hall, front; cellhouses, rear (Courtesy Joliet Area Historical Museum, Joliet, Illinois)

Fig. 21. The "opera house": one of Stateville's panopticons
(Courtesy Joliet Area Historical Museum, Joliet, Illinois)

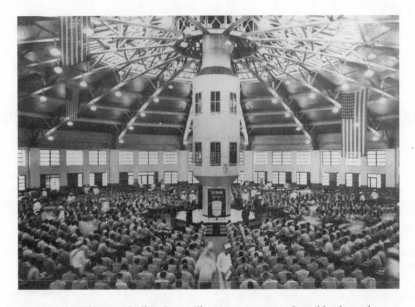

Fig. 22. The mess hall at Stateville, circa 1953: numbered backs and a
poster for *Roman Holiday*, the next show at the prison theater
(Courtesy Joliet Area Historical Museum, Joliet, Illinois)

Fig. 23. Birth of a monster: the new prison at Jackson, Michigan; inmates visible as dots around the ballpark (Courtesy Archives of Michigan)

Fig. 24. Putting down the riot, Jackson, 1952 (Courtesy Archives of Michigan)

Fig. 25. Two worlds, in sight of each other (Author's collection)

You Built It, Now Try to Run It

At the beginning and end of *20,000 Years in Sing Sing*, the audience sees shots of the real prison: aerial views of oppressive masses of brick and stone; footage of the institution observed from the river, looking like a heavy, gray, industrial town; a picture of hundreds of inmates herded together in front of the giant 1820s cellhouse. Added to these daunting images is a shot of inmates marching on the iron galleries of a stone cellblock, each wearing a drab prison uniform, each with his sentence superimposed on him in white letters: "10 Years," "23 Years," "45 Years"—sentences adding up to the disturbing total of 20,000 years for the prison as a whole. The repetition of these images locks in the movie's sense of enclosure. They are the kind of images that have been repeated in countless films, books, and television programs. And—minus the "Years" gimmick—they represent the real experience of generations of convicts. But they don't represent the whole experience. They suggest a world of total control, yet totality was an illusion. The Big House was America's greatest experiment in social planning, but one of the clearest results of the experiment was its proof of the individual's ability to resist.

It is interesting that radicals and reformers have been more tempted than conservatives to believe that this resistance can be contained, once the right container is found. Bentham and Foucault, the two prophets of the panopticon, are the best examples. Foucault may have regretted that panopticons (literal or symbolic) actually work, but he, like Bentham, was confident about their capacity to do so. Brockway had the same faith in his reformatory. The builders of Auburn, Cherry Hill, and Stateville felt the same about their penitentiaries. And anyone might think that a mammoth stone or concrete building, equipped with every means of restraint and punishment that an industrial civilization can provide and staffed by hundreds of people working to ensure that its inhabitants stay inside and conform to the rules, would have little trouble accomplishing its aim. Yet research inspired by Foucault's own theories routinely produces proof that total control and surveillance are, and always have been, illusory.[1] Beneath the appearance (and the reality) of regimentation, the Big House was usually in remarkable disorder. When convicts got out of hand, order was restored with brutality.[2] But they were always getting out of hand.

Even the history of Alcatraz, presumably America's most secure prison, can be told as a story of convicts getting drunk, making weapons, murdering fellow convicts, bribing officers to smuggle messages out and contraband in, sawing through the bars, wandering off into zones from which escapes could be made, climbing the perimeter fence, taking officers captive to cover their attempts to flee, and actually managing to flee. It wasn't the perfection of custody and surveillance that made their escape attempts result in recapture or death. They could, and did, escape the cells, the walls, and the fences, and reach the island's shore; but the frigid currents of San Francisco Bay thwarted or killed them all.[3]

Escape wasn't the inmates' only means of resisting Alcatraz. They repeatedly demonstrated their power by striking for better living conditions, and they sometimes succeeded. During one of their strikes, in 1937, an inmate attacked the warden, beat him unconscious, and used his head as a football. The victim somehow survived without severe injury, but the incident didn't reflect well on his total control of the total institution that Alcatraz was intended to be.[4] In 1946, six inmates tried to escape and failed; they then took over the cellhouse and held it for two days, using captured guards as hostages. The prison was recovered only after sustained artillery bombardment by marines and national guardsmen. Two officers and three convicts died.

The episode was startling, because it happened at Alcatraz. But uprisings and riots (or "mutinies," as they used to be called, as if prisoners were soldiers from whom loyalty might legitimately be expected) were normal events in the Big House. *O Pioneers!*

doesn't mention it, but while its author was working up the material for her novel, the Nebraska State Penitentiary was anything but the serenely rule-bound institution that appears in the book. A deputy warden was stabbed to death during a chapel service; a month later, three convicts escaped, shooting the warden, a second deputy warden, and another officer. The state militia was called in.[5] The incident caused a brief sensation, then was forgotten. But it was far from an unusual episode in American prison history.

The total institution wasn't really total, because no security or surveillance can be that way in a large and complicated institution. Gresham M. Sykes, a perceptive analyst of prisons, summarized the problem when he said that "the custodians are bound to their captives in a relationship of conflict rather than compelled acquiescence, despite the custodians' theoretical supremacy."[6] Nor did the custodians, unless insane, believe in their own "supremacy." Only the most theory-deluded reformers assumed, as Foucault apparently assumed, that practices of control and surveillance could impose so mightily on both captives and custodians that neither would understand the extent of their own, or the others', power. Models of society that proceed on the assumption that total control is possible are rendered ridiculous by the real experience of supposedly total institutions.

The Big House did not live by rules alone. Someone had to enforce the rules, and society had to pay to have them enforced—something it was reluctant to do. State legislatures might be willing to finance new and improved versions of the penitentiary, but when they did so, they often turned into monument builders, intent on erecting a really impressive institution, yet remaining stingy about its daily operations. They got what they paid for: poorly maintained buildings, outmoded security devices, and staffs that were often devoid of the training, morale, or motivation to manage a prison effectively.

Wardens were ordinarily appointed because their political party had won the last election, and removed when it lost the next one. Some had worked as sheriffs or other lawmen, but many had no relevant experience. Most weren't paid very well—as much, perhaps, as small-town high school superintendents are paid today—and they often shared the attitude of people who lived under communist regimes: "They pretend to pay us, and we pretend to work." Guards were grossly ill paid.[7] Their training often amounted to no more than a tour of the institution and the gift of a set of keys. Only a handful of dedicated senior officers, and a few young people who were interested in the challenge of learning how to run a prison, seem to have had any concept of professional standards.

Like the wardens, guards ordinarily didn't stay on the job very long; and while employed, many of them supplemented their income by resorting to corruption. Some wardens did too. In 1927 the former warden of the federal penitentiary at Atlanta had the special experience of starting a sentence in his own prison; he had accepted bribes from convicts and had gotten caught. His successor was so little trusted by his bosses in Washington that an undercover FBI agent was "sentenced" to Atlanta to investigate him (though the agent never found the evidence he was looking for).[8] Cars and convict servants, building supplies and farm goods had a way of drifting into the households of wardens and deputies, and sticking there. Some of these perquisites of office were regarded as legitimate forms of payment, and some were definitely not; but who, in that environment, was to insist on the rules?

In a typical prison, the warden's inmate favorites—his servants and clerks and musclemen, and the "con bosses" in the various departments—handled most of the institution's everyday business. No state wanted to pay civilians to drive the cars or keep the files. "Con-wise" officers understood the value of using inmates to manage other inmates. Inmates knew more about the job, and they could be cut adrift if things went wrong. Also, they worked cheap: the services of inmate "politicians" were compensated by other inmates. Men seeking a cell change or a better work assignment simply paid for it, with cigarettes, prison scrip, or gifts of a less tangible kind. Like the optimistic designers and reformers of the penitentiary, though with somewhat different intentions, the convict bosses and "operators" "made a world out of prison"—fully exploiting the possibilities of an artificial society.[9]

How much a warden knew about their dealings depended on how much he wanted to know. In most prisons, drugs and alcohol were accessible to anyone who could pay the price. Some contraband, such as low-grade alcoholic beverages ("pruno," for example), could be manufactured on the inside; the rest could be brought in by guards. Guns might also be smuggled in, commonly by inmates' civilian accomplices, but sometimes also by guards, defying their interest in their own safety.

In their more rational moments, wardens and officers realized that they were always vastly outnumbered by the convicts, and that there were always convicts who were ready to hurt them if they got the chance.[10] The response to this realization was usually accommodation and a degree of fraternization with the cons. By 1873 a new warden of Sing Sing was complaining that "officers and convicts mingle on a complete social basis."[11] When people have to live together, there is generally a pressure toward equality, especially when they come from similar social strata, as convicts and their virtually impoverished guards tended to do. Accounts of prison life often illustrate how far this kind of equality can go in repressing gratuitous sadism and aggression.

Nonetheless, and for obvious reasons, wealthy or prominent convicts were often accorded special privileges or attention. Despite the regimented life and the menial jobs that Al Capone endured at Alcatraz, he was treated with special concern by the staff—not, apparently, because he had money and was willing to distribute bribes, but because he was a famous gangster. As his prison doctor recalled, the officials' "interest in Capone was amazing. Alcatraz prisoners were considered equal, to be treated fairly, with no special favours. Their egos were to be deflated by exile to Alcatraz. Names in headlines and high-ranking public enemies were to be just numbers. Yet Capone was still the big shot, rating attention no other prisoner received."[12]

The length to which deference to fame can extend may be indicated by an episode from the late, decadent era of the Big House. Richard Speck, who was serving a life sentence in Stateville for the murder of eight women, died in 1991. Five years later, he was discovered to have starred in a video, produced inside the walls of the penitentiary, showing him using drugs, having sex with another inmate, and discussing his murders in a blasé tone. How could this have happened? One answer was supplied by an anonymous source, once associated with Stateville, who informed me that Speck was given latitude because he was famous—"because he was Richard Speck."[13]

But the primary reason why wardens as well as guards were anxious to come to terms with convicts, on a real though non-official basis, is simply that they were concerned for their own safety. Prison officers seldom fitted the cinematic tradition outrageously exemplified in *Shawshank:* they didn't strut around, advertising their masculinity and their contempt for inmates. They wouldn't have lasted long that way. The dramatic necessities of a prison are much subtler than those of a Hollywood movie, and the results of deviating from the script are much more serious.

Rightly or wrongly, America is a place where precedents are often ignored, but it is still surprising that some American historians depict "violence against guards and other staff members" as "extremely rare," before a strong surge in the 1960s and 1970s.[14] During the Big House period, guards and wardens were frequently assaulted or killed by convicts. So many wardens refused to appear in the yard without weapons or bodyguards, or a big, hungry dog, that boastful propaganda could be made on behalf of any warden who worked up the courage to go all the way Inside.

Frank Conley, longtime chief of the state prison at Deer Lodge, Montana, was a rough, mean man; but a contemporary remembered that "when a real tough prisoner came to Deer Lodge, Conley would assure him that if he behaved and caused no trouble he would see that he was paroled long before he otherwise would." No wonder: in 1908, when Conley was presiding over a prison court, an inmate killed Conley's assistant and gave Conley stab wounds that required forty stitches in the neck—"before the warden shot him." The inmate was quelled, and later executed, but Conley learned his lesson. Afterward he made certain accommodations.[15] It was good for him that he was given time to adjust. Other prison officials didn't fare so well.

Like the Nebraska state pen, the Massachusetts State Prison had bad luck with its chapel services. At the end of one of them, the deputy warden was stabbed to death on the speakers' platform. A few years later, a gang of prisoners, attempting to start a general riot, interrupted the chaplain's prayer and started carving up another deputy. The warden stopped them with his revolver. Another Massachusetts warden wasn't that fortunate; inmates waylaid him in a workshop and killed him. Similar things happened in many other Big Houses. At the Connecticut State Prison, two wardens in a row were killed, another was attacked with a hammer by one prisoner and seriously wounded with a knife by another, and a deputy warden was assaulted with an ax and nearly killed, all within a short period of time. In 1915, at Joliet, something new appeared in the record of Big House violence: an inmate valet murdered the warden's wife.[16]

Wardens sometimes proclaimed, rather than confessed, their inability to control the convicts. Sing Sing's Warden Lawes remarked complacently that "most attempts to escape are made by hiding out in the yard, which is not so difficult, as the area of the yard comprises twenty acres." By *yard* he meant the entire prison. The area was only about the size of five city blocks, but it offered plenty of opportunities for concealment. Lawes added that "one [escaping] prisoner died in his hiding place, and his skeleton was accidentally found ten years later." The warden was proud to report that only about three convicts a year now managed to escape from his prison—down from ten a year, five decades before. Sing Sing had roughly seventeen hundred inmates at the time, so its escape rate may seem negligible. One may wonder, though, why any inmates were permitted to leave.[17]

In 1941 the California Institution for Men was opened as a "prison without walls." Its escape rate during its first decade was 3 percent a year. The escape rate from the "wall-less" federal prison at Seagoville, Texas, was 1 percent in 1952. That compares well with the record of some prisons *with* walls. During one year in the 1950s, the Montana State Prison had an escape rate of 4.4 percent. In the 1970s the West Virginia Penitentiary averaged 3.7 percent annually; in 1974, 32.5 percent of the state's total prison population escaped. Another standout in this respect was the Indiana State Prison at Jeffersonville, which in its early days had an escape rate of 17 percent. The rate subsequently went down to a mere 8 percent.[18]

Jackson Prison, in the old days, was another institution with laughable security. On August 3, 1882, the night captain reported that number 1300, Smith, a lifer, had escaped through a skylight, heaving a chisel at the captain and thumbing his nose as he vanished over the roof. The captain may have been indulging his taste for irony when he wrote that "it has been quite a while since we've had an escape," because this was far from an uncommon incident. He had just reported an escape on July 18, and some good tries on June 17 and July 21—not to mention a serious attempt on July 28 to burn the prison down. Jackson's level of security is suggested by the fact that it possessed only one pair of handcuffs, repaired with baling wire. A decade after the night captain's report, a convict treated a gatekeeper at Jackson to a pitcher of poisoned lemonade, then escaped, leaving the officer dead behind him.[19]

Another Michigan prison, located at Marquette in the arctic Upper Peninsula, was known as the state's Siberia, notorious for rigid discipline. Yet its history is a virtually continuous record of murders, mass escapes from inside the walls, walkaways by convicts trusted to work outside, and the introduction of sensible security techniques only after some phenomenal breach of security had occurred. There were innumerable dramatic moments in an environment in which dramatic moments were not supposed to happen.

In 1921 inmates being treated to a movie jumped the warden and other officers, stabbed them, and chased the warden through the prison, trying to finish him off. Amid scenes that would seem ridiculous in the most ridiculous western, the elderly warden fought for his life. His attackers were routed at last by one officer and one inmate, who seized a gun and knew what to do with it; but the warden and a deputy died from the wounds they had already received. In 1939 another warden, his deputy, and two members of the parole board were kidnapped by would-be escapees who got the drop on them at a meeting inside the walls. When the convicts and their captives arrived at the prison gate, the guard said, "Warden, you are the very man who told me that no one taken hostage has any authority. My job is on the line." The warden said, "Your job is not in jeopardy, Paddy, but mine is. Open the gate." The gate opened, and the inmates went off with their hostages—to be recaptured after a long, thrilling chase. It was a charming incident, in its way. Less charming was the attempt of inmates to escape by kidnapping the state governor when he made the mistake of visiting the prison's mess hall in 1950. A wild battle erupted as the governor and his party struggled against inmates armed with knives and vegetable mashers. It was brought to an end when a state police bodyguard used a gun that he had smuggled inside the prison in violation of its rules.[20]

Marquette was hardly an exception when it came to escape attempts involving public officials. In 1935 San Quentin, a formerly "reformed" prison, was spiraling out of control. An officer was stabbed; guns were manufactured on the premises; whiskey was for sale on the yard at five dollars a pint. Then four convicts entered the warden's residence with smuggled guns, beat and kicked him nearly to death, and forced the members of the parole board, with whom he had been lunching, to strip and exchange clothes with them. With the board as hostages, the convicts persuaded guards to open the gate, and they escaped in the warden's car. Later that day, one of them was killed and the others recaptured; two were executed.[21]

In 1937, seven escapees seized the warden of California's Folsom Prison, which was smaller but reputedly tougher than San Quentin, and demanded that the tower guards give them weapons. This warden had told the guards, "If I am ever kidnapped and I order you not to shoot and you obey my order, you won't be here the next day. No matter what I tell you, you start shooting." That's what they did, while the warden and two fellow captives tried to fight off the prisoners. The warden and one of his officers were knifed to death. In 1929 inmates at the Colorado State Penitentiary captured a cellhouse, took guards hostage, and started executing them as a means of persuading the warden to facilitate their escape. He refused. The Catholic chaplain tried to dynamite a hole in the cellhouse wall, but, true to Big House ideals, the wall refused to budge, although the blast "rocked the whole town." Finally, with "machine gun bullets . . . pour[ing] through the windows by the thousands," the leading rebels committed suicide, and the affair was over, leaving a dozen people dead.[22]

In the same year, and in the now-familiar Big House style, inmates at Auburn obtained arms and took the warden hostage. They got him to pass out a note telling his officers to let them escape. The state's acting governor was not encouraging. "The warden will have to take his chances," he said. State troopers moved in with gas bombs and gunfire, rescued the warden, chased the convicts into their cellblock fortifications, and shot them down, one by one. Nine convicts and one officer died. Governor Franklin Roosevelt, who was traveling during the incident, fully approved the decisions of Acting Governor Herbert H. Lehman.[23]

It must be stipulated that the consequences of escape attempts were more likely to be comic than tragic. Convicts who got past the wall usually wandered about aimlessly until they were caught. They put all their thoughts into escaping, not into the problem of what to do thereafter. But their adventures showed how hard it is to keep even unreflective people in a place where they don't want to be. The U.S. penitentiary at Marion, Illinois, succeeded Alcatraz as the federal prison system's warehouse for its hardest cases. To leave the institution, one had to pass through three gates, not just the normal two; and everything was controlled by the latest electronic devices. But in 1973, five inmates figured out how to insert an "override" mechanism into the equipment. They walked blithely through the gates—only to be caught and returned, because they hadn't planned what they would do once they got out.[24]

No comedy could be distilled, however, from the sickening events at the Ohio State Penitentiary in 1930. Inmates set a fire, either as an act of protest or as a means of covering an escape; the fire spread quickly, and more than three hundred men, trapped in their cells, were killed. The disaster, one of the worst fires in American history, was followed by more than a week of rioting, in which inmates captured and wrecked much of the prison that had survived. Given the lax administration of most penitentiaries, it's a miracle that horrors of this magnitude were rare.

Riots were not. By one specialist's conservative reckoning, there were 199 serious disturbances in American prisons from 1855 to 1955; at least twelve times, riots occurred in series, in one institution after another. In the 1917–52 period, particularly "large and serious riots" happened more than once every two years.[25] Riots started in so many ways that even the best authorities found it hard to generalize about them. The immediate cause might be an unsuccessful escape attempt, a psychotic's sudden chance to seize a guard, a food complaint in the mess hall, a confrontation between an officer and an inmate on a work assignment, a quarrel between two inmates in the yard, a botched attempt to punish an inmate—anything, in short, might set things off.

Some causes have varied over time. Today antagonisms among ethnically identified convict gangs represent a major source of prison violence. That wasn't true about the Big House period, although ethnic issues weren't without significance. In 1914, when black inmates constituted less than 10 percent of San Quentin's population, they made a bold attempt to end racial segregation in the mess hall by mounting a hunger strike. It failed. When administrators themselves tried to outlaw segregation in 1945, they were vanquished by hunger strikes on the opposite side, and a race riot.[26] Ethnic violence also occurred between Mexican inmates and others. In 1925, when the Mexican population at San Quentin approached 25 percent, the prison was convulsed by a series of murders and riots involving Mexicans and Anglos. Nevertheless, as a good historian of San Quentin has observed, virtually all the riots between 1880 and 1950 were about a more basic subject: food.[27]

But that conveys too simple an impression. Ordinarily, no single problem, no single, dramatic incident has the power to convulse an entire prison. Experts maintain that there must be a set of underlying institutional conditions—some combination of inadequate staff, frustrating procedures, lack of work, lack of recreation, lack of psychological counseling and appropriate classification, or the seemingly eternal problem, "overcrowding"—before a riot takes place. Some observers point to a common cycle in prison management: first, officials transfer their authority to con bosses; then they wonder whether the transfer has gone too far; finally they try to take their power back, thus upsetting the system and inciting an insurrection.[28]

The difficulty is that any of these causes may easily continue to be "underlying," or merely troublesome, and not produce a riot. A plausible theory asserts that two major conditions must be met before a riot takes place: a breakdown in administration and a breakdown in security. The administrative breakdown might have to do with anything from conflicts among officials to the existence of a pervasive sense of unfairness among inmates—whatever would make the administration be seen as no longer legitimate. When a bad administration is combined (as it often is) with bad security—poor equipment, lax procedures, untrained officers—the stage is set for riot.[29]

So goes the theory, which is strongly supported by the history of riots during the Big House period. What it doesn't explain is why badly managed prisons didn't have still more riots. There may not be an answer to that question, even a book-length answer. Convicts can be regimented, oppressed, overcrowded, and poorly guarded, but they remain individuals. No one can assemble all the causes and calculate all the odds for individual choices in a multitude of specific situations. Further, even a Big House that was indifferently run had many means, besides the walls and bars, of preserving a semblance of order.

One means was the convicts themselves. A writer on super–maximum security units observes that inmates can manipulate their keepers simply by appearing to obey all the rules[30]—and to appear to obey is often to obey in fact. If the keepers are manipulated into providing some reward in return for obedience, both parties to the implicit bargain may be satisfied with the exchange. More significant: many of the same inmates who naturally resist the institution in any way they can, day by day, also tend to resist trouble in the institution. A former warden has said that convicts "are really tolerant. Really, really tolerant. . . . You can establish almost any type of rule but as long as you consistently enforce it and explain it, they'll end up accepting it. . . . They feel sort of helpless in that regard. A high percentage, whether 95 or whatever, don't want any trouble." This implies, of course, that "there's 5 percent who aren't tolerant," and they need special security—but, as this expert suggests, a warden who can't deal with that 5 percent should be held responsible for almost anything that goes wrong in his prison.[31]

Some of the other means by which prison maintains itself fall into the general category of "safety valves" (a common metaphor in prison writing). One of the "valves" in the Big House was the unspoken policy of ensuring that most convicts didn't spend an extremely long time in prison—the policy, to use another metaphor, of making prison a revolving door. In the nineteenth-century Big House, pardons were common, and a "life" sentence often meant "only a few years."[32] And short prison terms weren't just a feature of the early days. The 1880 census estimated that the average stay in prison was around two to two and a half years; in 1960 it was twenty-eight months, with a median of twenty-one months. In 1952 authorities announced that lifers in American prisons served an average of ten years or less.[33] Wherever admissions statistics for the Big House period can be checked for a long series of years, the pattern of short stays shows up.

One snapshot illustrates the pattern. In 1954 inmates of the New Jersey State Prison at Trenton were such a bad bunch, on the whole, that 24 percent of them had been sentenced for felonious homicide. The vast majority were recidivists. Yet half had been in prison for only two years or less on their current sentences.[34] In *Brute Force* (1947), a better-than-average prison movie, an aggrieved convict shouts at the warden: "Those gates only open three times: when you come in, when you've served your time, or when you're dead!" True, in a way; but the image was a lot more brutal than the reality.

In 1947, indeed, the concept of the "time" you "serve" was changing, under the influence of "progressive" ideas—although, as it happened, the changes weren't wholly for the better. Progressive penology's favorite means of dealing with release from prison were good time, parole, and the indeterminate sentence ("three years to life"), all of which promised reduction of prison time in return for proper "adjustment" to prison—a real as well as a verbal paradox, since adjustment to prison is not the same as adjustment to life. Parole and the indeterminate sentence probably increased tensions more than diminished them, because inmates believed that decisions about their adjustment and release were strange and capricious. From the 1930s on, prisons expanded their academic and vocational schools and began hiring psychologists and sociologists to implement schemes of "individual treatment" to equip prisoners for release. Inmates were periodically interviewed and counseled, and programs of many kinds were instituted to "rehabilitate" them. But the counseling was often perfunctory, and the programs—art, addiction recovery, college correspondence courses—would have been more beneficial if convicts hadn't seen them chiefly as ways of piling up favorable evidence for the almighty parole board, whose secret deliberations were bewildering and frustrating.[35]

Other, less mystical, safety valves included a variety of new "privileges" that came with the twentieth century: movies, radios, inmate newspapers, well-stocked commissaries. Such privileges supplemented traditional, though frequently less respectable, means of rewarding prisoners for their cooperation: desirable jobs; tacit permission for drugs and drink, sex and petty pilfering; and the appointment of "operators" and "politicians," who might otherwise be "troublemakers," to positions in which they could order other inmates around. Those were real rewards, and they contributed greatly to the maintenance of the Big House.

So much for rewards. What about punishments—the means of institutional self-preservation most closely associated with the image of the Big House?

This is another complex issue. In the nineteenth century, "rehabilitation," as it is now called, did not exclude "physical violence." The two belonged together, as two parts of the total institution. At the Michigan State Prison, men were casually taken out and "given a touch of the 'bat'"—for the crime of refusing to attend school. The physical discipline of "reformatories" was little different from that of "penitentiaries." Superintendent Brockway was a champion of reform, not just of individuals but also of penal institutions; yet he didn't hesitate to beat his young convicts at Elmira Reformatory. When they got out of line they were spanked on their bare buttocks with a quarter-inch strap, soaked in water to make it heavier. There was an average of 516 spankings a year, and the average number of blows per spanking was 7.56 (good records were kept). Joseph Pulitzer's populist *New York World* found out about this and campaigned frantically against the great penologist and reformer, representing him as the devil incarnate. In response, sympathetic newspapers reported that only 29 percent of Elmira's inmates had been spanked.[36] From this battle of reformers versus reformers, Brockway—supported, as reformers often are, by wealthy and influential friends—emerged victorious. But his scandal was a sign of things to come.

The next two generations saw the gradual, grudging abolition of corporal punishment in Big Houses around the country. Psychological substitutes were discovered, especially isolation and loss of privileges. Many prisoners, however, would undoubtedly have preferred being hit with a nightstick to being denied visits from their families, or being kicked off the baseball team. Psychological punishment isn't necessarily more humane than corporal punishment—or more effective in maintaining order. But humanitarian feeling had progressed so far that America was no longer psychologically prepared to face the continuance of corporal punishment. In 1907 the warden of Delaware's prison at Wilmington resigned rather than continue to whip the inmates: "'I would rather hang a man for murder!' he burst out, smashing the top of his desk with a brawny hand. . . . 'My feelings have been awful beyond description.'" The newspaper headline was "Wanted—A Heartless Man," the man who would dare to take the sympathetic warden's place.[37]

It is convenient to believe that what we regard as moral is also practical. In a society with an officially humanitarian ethic, even experts on the practical difficulties of running a prison often assert that "brutal" methods of punishment have never really "worked." Modern Americans set such a high moral value on the abolition of suffering in general that when specific suffering occurs, they assume that something must have gone wrong, something that might easily have gone right. Donald Clemmer understood the way in which humanitarian ideas that seem to work on the Outside are eventually, and almost automatically, adopted as standards for what should happen on the Inside. He knew that this transformation of outside expectations into inside rules may not always be appropriate. He also knew, and emphasized, that inmates naturally break the rules that are made for them. Yet he spoke of "the utter futility" of all the usual methods of enforcing rules through punishment—even such a relatively light punishment as solitary confinement. He may have meant that punishment was futile in reforming people. But reformation isn't the only function of punishment, and he ignored the possibility that it might be useful in restraining people who naturally object to restraint.[38]

John Bartlow Martin, the 1950s' most dedicated reporter on the prison beat, made a similar confession of humanitarian faith. He related an episode from a riot in the New Jersey penitentiary. The warden told shouting inmates that if they didn't stop, he would make an example of one of them. They didn't stop, so he selected a man who was pounding on the bars of his cell and had him beaten. "The noise in that wing," says Martin's source, "immediately stopped." Martin's conclusion: "Force has not been proved efficacious in handling prisoners."[39] That was patently untrue, on his own evidence.

Strange statements have been made on the other side, too. Lord Wellington, the victor of Waterloo, said that you can't have an army without discipline, and you can't have discipline without punishment, and "there is no punishment which makes an impression upon anybody except corporal punishment." He also was obviously wrong. It is impossible to imagine a large institution that can be commanded simply by physical force. Even Captain Lynds, the demonic creator of Sing Sing, was famous for getting obedience through his dark personal charisma, not just his whippings.[40]

The usefulness of respect, persuasion, cooperation, and accommodation becomes starkly apparent wherever the bosses are overwhelmingly outnumbered by the bossed, as they were in the

Big House. Clearly, some kind of working relationship has to be established between the keepers and the kept. It can be created by consistent rules, an appearance of fairness, the hope of a shortened "jolt" behind bars if one obeys the rules, and the threat of punishment, timely and judicious, if one fails to do so. It can be created by an intelligent allotment of legitimate privileges, or of the enjoyment of power and vice, as gifts of the deputy warden. Whatever form it takes, the trick is to get the convicts to do more of what you want, with a smaller application of direct force.

The normal condition of the Big House—soulless regimentation on the surface, soulful turbulence underneath—shows how hard the trick was to master. Most experts thought that truly large prisons, prisons containing more than, say, fifteen hundred men, could be operated in some fashion (after all, they remained in business), but they could never be managed with real success.[41] Next we will examine a very large Big House where most things actually were, for a long time, very well managed. We will also examine a Big House where, for a long time, almost everything went wrong—ridiculously, embarrassingly, violently wrong.

SEVEN

A Tale of Two Prisons

In the early twentieth century, two midwestern states built prisons that were regarded as the biggest of all Big Houses: Stateville (Illinois) and Jackson (Michigan).[1] Stateville opened officially in 1925, when Jackson was under construction and soon to open. Each of these two great "cities" had walls enclosing more than two and a half million square feet—twice the size of the Pentagon. And at the beginning, Stateville was an even bigger mess than Jackson.

When Joseph Ragen became warden in 1935, Stateville was run by the convicts, if it was run at all. The yard housed a village of eighty-three wooden shacks—a Grand Bazaar of inmate clubs and stores where liquor was dispensed, gambling casinos were operated, and young men were sold as sex toys. Some of the acreage was devoted to marijuana cultivation. Inmates crammed their cells with overstuffed chairs and put curtains over the bars to ensure privacy from prying guards. Cells hosted cats, dogs, rabbits, and canaries—as many as two hundred birds per cell, bred for the pet shop market. Pigeons were raised for cooking on improvised stoves. Vermin reveled in the storerooms and kitchen. Escapes were common. Untrained and ill-paid officers were easily bribed and intimidated by prison gangs.[2] In 1926 the deputy warden was stabbed to death when he declined to assist inmates who were trying to escape. Five years later a massive riot broke out, sparked by another escape attempt. The world's most modern prison was said to have reached a point where "the inmates have established their own unofficial version of control," and the guards "have withdrawn to the walls." That phrase, which frequently recurs in the prison literature, designates the stage of institutional degradation at which the only thing that makes the Big House look like a separate world is its concrete shell.[3] Pleased with the architecture of the model prison they had built, state officials abdicated responsibility for running it.

Ragen (1897–1971) took more than a decade to consolidate his control. He razed the Grand Bazaar, put gang leaders in isolation, fired incompetent guards, and gradually placed his own men in every assignment in the prison. He made himself so crucial to the maintenance of order that his regime became untouchable by the state's political parties. It was Ragen, not convict gangs, clerks, or bosses, who governed his penitentiary. He created a staff that was completely under his thumb, and he treated it, in some ways, as if its members were convicts. As the best historian of his career has said, "the basis of his control was punishment: whenever a mistake occurred, a guard was punished." Convicts averaged about five "beefs" a year; guards about one—not a big number, but significant in a professional organization.[4] Most of the offenses were minor, and so were most of the punishments: temporary loss of privileges (for convicts), temporary loss of pay (for officers); but at Stateville, rules were enforced. Praising Ragen's regime, a national magazine cheerfully revealed that "guards, like inmates, are spied on."[5] And like the inmates, the guards knew who was boss.

The average tenure of guards at Stateville was about one year. That looks bad, but its true meaning is that officers who didn't adapt to Ragen's operation soon went elsewhere, while those who did adapt enjoyed the opportunity of climbing the bureaucratic ladder and joining his "praetorian guard of lieutenants ceaselessly prowling the prison."[6] By conforming to the Stateville code, with all its demands for discipline and all its threats of punishment and humiliation, officers attained a quietly professionalized yet potent masculinity. Inmates also had an incentive to adapt, and their reward, though less agreeable, was more important: they were safe. As Ragen realized, most people will adapt to a regime that gives them safety, especially when they have no prospect of getting anything better. His accomplishment was to reduce to an absolute minimum the robberies, rapes, attacks, and murders that both penologists and the American public have often accepted as inevitable features of prison life.

Ragen tried to mythologize himself as a man who by unique and mysterious talents achieved a practically perfect record of control at Stateville. That wasn't true. Discipline sometimes broke down. In 1949 there was a disturbance in the mess hall, accompanied by what internal reports describe as a "demonstration" in the cellhouses, with convicts rattling their doors, throwing things, and shouting "fuck that meatball, the son-of-a-bitch is no good and he never will be."[7] Ragen's nickname was "Meatball," because he looked like one.

He was fat, ugly, and self-congratulating. He was a worshiper of the dullest of deities, bureaucracy. Yet he controlled his Big House as well as any large institution has ever been controlled, and far better than any other Big House. He came as close as anyone could to fulfilling Foucault's theories about universal control. He was the best evidence for the theories, but he was also the best evidence against them, because he demonstrated that the great web of panopticons couldn't run itself, no matter what its effects on the consciousness of inmates and officers. Someone of cunning and fortitude had to struggle constantly to run it, always against strong odds. The means of surveillance and the tools of discipline wouldn't perform the task; those had existed before Joseph Ragen, and they didn't work. Only he could do it.

His was a triumph as enormous as Stateville itself—a triumph resulting from his fanatical pettiness, his determination that convicts be constantly watched, searched, and counted, that their possessions be severely limited, that their movements be meticulously monitored by tickets and time stamps and an "avalanche of forms," and that their keepers never make "the slightest oversight" in performing their humdrum duties—because, in the Big House, the slightest oversight can have devastating consequences.[8] As one convict said, Ragen had "no pals among inmates."[9] Yet by enforcing a framework of rules, he made their lives secure.

Ragen was no deep thinker, but he had an intelligent concern with his job. He identified what needed to be controlled, and he devised means of controlling it. Knowing that riots are more likely to happen in the mess hall than anywhere else, he made sure that Stateville would never, not for a moment, run out of good food. Knowing that it's a security risk to involve large numbers of inmates in school or vocational education, he sent them to school anyway—and put sufficient resources into monitoring them. Most important, he stayed on the job, watching over his forms and regulations. That's what interested him, and that's what he was good at. His reward was seeing even liberal journalists admire Stateville as "America's Toughest Prison," tougher than Alcatraz.[10]

Quite different interests seem to have motivated the wardens who ran (or rather, did *not* succeed in running) Jackson Prison.[11] The "State Prison of Southern Michigan," built as a replacement for the old Victorian joint in downtown Jackson, was the capital of its own kingdom—five thousand acres of swamps and streams, woods and farms, houses for officers and far-flung barracks for convict laborers. Seen from a distance, the prison itself looked like a splendid new Ford factory, the best work of Albert Kahn or some other modern industrial architect. It appeared to be a generously proportioned one- or two-story building, full of big windows and faced with fine brickwork. But coming closer, one grasped its scale: the "single-story" facade was fifty feet tall and a third of a mile long; the windows were sheeted with bars, and behind them were rows of cages stacked five stories high.

The deceptive facade was an appropriate symbol. This beautiful modern prison was never what it appeared to be. Jacktown was the scene of fantastic corruption and stupidity. Inmates were customarily allowed to wander freely around their cellblocks, and often from block to block. Every day, thousands were released into the yard at the same time and permitted to do whatever occurred to them. Convicts in the metalworking shop made knives to order for paying customers, and guards did a good business importing drugs and liquor. There was also a domestic production: a quart of homemade brew sold for fifteen to twenty packs of cigarettes, retail—not a bad price for contraband. It is said, with slight exaggeration, that "bushels of empty whisky and rum bottles clogged the sewers of 16-block."[12]

At Jackson, cell searches were haphazard and lethargic; the place was understaffed, and besides, who cared? Security wasn't a high priority. Inmates were permitted to block their bars with cardboard, rendering supervision impossible. They were allowed to buy commissary goods in glass jars, which could easily be broken into weapons. As late as 1951 they were allowed to keep canaries, creatures that dirtied the cells and provided yet another obstacle to effective searches. "The fellows love 'em," said Michigan's genial commissioner of corrections. "I couldn't see any harm in their having one apiece." The same penological czar announced that he couldn't see any harm in convicts' having money, "though all prisons forbid it." They forbid it so that convicts will have a harder time loan-sharking, bribing their guards, and buying sex and drugs. In the 1940s and early 1950s, Jackson's favored convicts followed the institutional custom of driving around southern Michigan in prison vehicles—running errands, going to ballgames, and visiting bars. Other inmates paid taxi drivers or guards to take them to houses of prostitution: "two bushels of potatoes [from the prison farm] would get the best prostitute in Jackson."[13]

The prison was a classic example of inmate control. Civilians managed what might be called the institution's foreign policy, its relations with state officials, business leaders, and bigwigs generally, while convict clerks and other members of the prison intelligentsia made the really important decisions: work assignments, cell assignments, basic services to their fellow inmates. The best organized of the convicts, the members of criminal gangs, naturally rose to the top. Much has been said about the value of the convict boss system as a method of social control—roughly the same that has been said about the boss system as a method of social control in big-city politics. As one Michigan official observed in the early 1950s, "Convicts know more about prisons than anybody else. They know how to run them. In the old days we used to say if you let the inmates run it, it'll be all right."[14] Inmates at Jackson ran a pay-to-play system: you could pay for peace; you could pay for sex; you could pay for anything—except for a system that wasn't run by criminals.

Presumably, almost everybody knew what was going on. Only occasionally would a staff member show his ignorance of the fact that he was playing the buffoon in a farce written by the inmates. In 1934 Albert Merritt Ewert, a Protestant chaplain at Jackson, made himself the laughingstock of the state by inviting eighteen convicts—gangsters and others who were notoriously "hep to the drift"—to a Thanksgiving celebration at his home. When the newspapers reported this, they also reported that Ewert had dressed a convict in civilian clothes and put him in charge of the prison's news service. Journalists objected to dealing with a convict as if he were a press secretary, but prison authorities backed him up, until he failed to appear at his next news conference—because he had escaped from prison. Other embarrassments occurred. On Christmas Eve, Ewert's houseboy, who had been a guest at the Thanksgiving dinner, "climaxed an investigation" into drug dealing to other inmates by making his own escape.[15]

Ewert's long-term accomplishment was the use of his influence to secure the appointment as deputy warden of a man whose chief qualifications were his popularity among inmates and his status as Ewert's "right-hand man." (Ewert suggested that the inmates would have rioted if the appointment hadn't been made.) This affable fellow, D. C. Pettit, was probably the most corrupt official at the prison. We will soon see more of Officer Pettit. Ewert, locked in his good intentions, never realized that he was making a distinguished contribution to Jackson's corruption. His friendly convict helpers kept an elaborate scrapbook of newspaper stories about him, the majority so damaging that only an invincibly self-convinced personality could have endured the pain of reading them.[16]

Ewert wasn't alone in his naiveté. When Lewis Lawes inspected Jacktown in 1943, he complimented its modern facilities but reserved his highest praise for its atmosphere. "The talking and laughing and yelling [in the dining hall] was just like you'd find outside anywhere. It wasn't like prison. . . . It has the closest thing to a normal atmosphere that I've found anywhere."[17]

The "normal atmosphere" at Jackson had some interesting effects. On January 11, 1945, Warren Hooper, a state senator who was about to testify in a corruption probe, was ambushed and murdered twenty miles up the road from the prison. The case was never officially solved, but evidence indicated that Hooper was slain by three inmate members of Detroit's Purple Gang, with the help of Deputy Warden Pettit's stylish coupe, lent to the convicts for the occasion. A headline-grabbing investigation portrayed the prison as a den of "rackets" and "sex perversion."[18] The warden, Harry Jackson, who had helped to build the penitentiary, was contemptuously dismissed, together with Pettit and other members of his staff.

Two years later, there was another inquiry into corruption at the prison. The new warden, Ralph Benson, refused to compel inmates to go across the road and appear before investigators at the state police post. Defending his action (or inaction), he summarized the problems of control and accommodation that were endemic to the Big House: "We have got to live with those boys in there, and if I force a man to come over here, and he gets mad at me, I have got to meet him in the yard and in the dining room. You just don't understand." That was true, so far as it went; although a little later in the warden's testimony it was discovered that he had "a very pronounced odor of liquor" on his breath. Within the prison, he had been viewed as a strict disciplinarian. Perhaps he was—by Jackson's standards.[19]

Benson's successor was Julian Frisbie, a career officer in the Marine Corps. More discipline was probably expected from him, but it was during his administration that the riot of 1952 took place, a revolt that ranks with the insurrection at Attica as the biggest in American history. As we have seen, an inmate in the segregation block beguiled a young, ill-trained guard and used his keys to free the other convicts on the block. Rioting, which was initially confined to a single building, spread to the rest of the prison when Frisbie fecklessly decided to let the remaining inmates proceed to the mess hall instead of feeding them in their cells, which he feared might provoke their anger. All went well until an inmate stood up and yelled, "There's salt in the coffee." The mess hall exploded, and the guards fled for their lives.[20]

Soon thousands of convicts were running free, burning the laundry, library, and chapel, trashing the cellhouses. The warden confessed that he "didn't know what to do" with his "untrained guards," so the state police moved in. Killing one inmate and firing over the others' heads, they drove the rioters back into the cells. Three days later, the prison's sociologist persuaded the inmates still barricaded in the segregation block to surrender without hurting the eight guards they retained as hostages. The big riot was over. Ten weeks afterward, however, inmates in one of the blocks escaped from their cells by bending the lightweight bars with their hands. They captured guards and had to be subdued by state police. A new warden was appointed, and he finally organized a riot squad among his officers. Much of the prison was still in ruins when yet another riot started in the mess hall. This time, the riot squad entered, guns blazing, and put it down.[21]

The ridiculous events at Jackson prompted further, embarrassing inquiries. The commissioner of corrections, who appears to have been a well-intentioned dope, was asked about the special treatment he had given an inmate. "I have no personal preferences here," he replied. "They are fellows I like. They're all good boys. A lot of fellows I would like to see out but I can't get them out and I shan't. It is my job to keep them all happy." The inmate in question, Philip Keywell, was a leader in the gang that had liquidated Senator Hooper. He had been named in a preceding investigation as one of the con bosses who ran the rackets in Jackson's hospital, and who had considered liquidating the state governor. "What a joke it would be," he said, "about the world's largest prison."[22]

The target of this joke was the pride evoked by Jackson's size. Even the inmates couldn't resist that pride. As late as the 1990s Jackson's inmate newspaper proudly proclaimed itself "The Spectator: Serving the World's Largest Prison." Keywell's escapade would have shown that size wasn't everything. Ironically, penological experts and state riot investigators agreed with him. They regarded Jackson's grand dimensions as its greatest defect; they bewailed the prison's "excessive size" and pronounced it "impossible to administer."[23] But the deeper irony was that the "world's largest prison" didn't need to be a joke. It might have been run right. The task could have been accomplished only by a rare enthusiast like Ragen, a virtuoso of seemingly petty details. But it might have been done.

Even Ragen would have admitted that the larger the institution, the taller the pyramid of officers that are needed to run it, and the more complicated the problems that necessarily result. But few prison workers will quarrel with the judgment of old Zebulon Brockway, who asserted that only a small minority of prisoners are "intractable."[24] The majority are willing to accommodate themselves to prison—and they do so, in one way or another. The goal is to get them to do that, without, as old-line prison officers said, "giving the place away," and without neglecting the possibility that prison might have some usefulness for prisoners who are not "intractable."

This is where the reformers, and the heroes of prison management, come in.

EIGHT

Rajahs and Reformers

The Big House wouldn't be the Big House if it weren't for the many people who have tried to reform it. The institution owed its existence to reform. The penitentiary was conceived as a modern and humane replacement for public, crude, physically painful punishments. Half a century after the opening of the penitentiaries at Auburn and Cherry Hill, the construction of Zebulon Brockway's Elmira Reformatory inaugurated the era of the Big House proper, an institution that was not only punitive but (purportedly) educational, not only large but (purportedly) total. It resulted from a movement to reform the penitentiary as it had developed and make it work toward the actual reform of its inmates. The reforming spirit manifested itself in eccentric individualists, the most interesting of whom not only criticized the Big House but also took responsibility for running it.

Brockway (1827–1920), Elmira's rajah of reform, was a paragon of eccentricity. An intelligent and, in his way, a sensitive man, he was influenced by memories of youthful misdeeds and of a father who beat him, then "relentingly" demanded to be beaten in return. This, for some reason, reformed the son, who concluded that individual character and choice are "predetermined" by influences "beyond the individual control." That idea, which he held to be unassailable, led him to hope that convicts could be reformed if they were confined within a total institution where keepers could "invade the will of those committed to our charge and determine their behavior quite outside their own election."[1]

One of the earliest true prison professionals, a man with a real sense of vocation, Brockway worked his way up various institutional ladders and in 1876 happily accepted an invitation to govern Elmira, then under construction. There he organized what he called a "scientific cultural system of regeneration." What this meant in practice was that Elmira's young inmates (aged sixteen to thirty, the big years for crime) were supervised with Bentham-like zeal, their every act of obedience or defiance marked and recorded, so that Brockway could decide who would ascend or descend in "grade," or perhaps be allowed, at last, to leave Elmira. His great principles, as summarized by Lewis Lawes, were "secure custody," "no outside influence or interference," an executive "with wide discretionary powers," and a regime in which the "entire life of the prisoner should be directed; all waking hours and activities, bodily and mental habits, also his emotional exercises."[2]

Lawes thought this "an admirable program," and any manager of a large enterprise might instinctively agree ("wide discretionary powers"!). Yet whether Elmira's discipline achieved "entirety" is very doubtful. Brockway thought it did, but only such an eccentric individualist could preserve his faith in the absolute rightness of any scheme he happened to come up with. Brockway planned Elmira as a place where inmates would be reformed by doing real work that would earn real money, money that would incidentally help to keep the prison going. Then laws were passed outlawing prison industries as injurious to competition. So Brockway turned to military drill as his inmates' chief occupation, and satisfied himself that this was an even better idea than the original one. He built a vast drill hall, with an acre of marching space. He invited crowds of visitors into his prison to witness his success in making toy soldiers out of thieves and rapists. The "military" exercises at Elmira were the delight of the hinterland, and of Brockway himself, despite the expense, and the frustration of his initial and rational intentions.[3]

The Elmira Reformatory issued elaborate reports, full of pictures and case studies of inmates in the process of rehabilitation. Yet in these volumes, the methods of reform—military drill, industrial training (some of which Brockway was able to keep at Elmira), high school courses, philosophical lectures, whatever else—seem much less important than the impression of uniforms, parade grounds, monumental walls, and small, serially numbered young men. To the twenty-first-century observer, Elmira doesn't *look* like a paradise of humanitarian reform; it looks like the apotheosis of prudish discipline. But humanitarian motives have led to stranger destinations than this.

The discovery that Brockway had learned the use of corporal punishment, that he believed in it, and that he practiced it on a grand scale came as a shock to many people even in his own time. It still registers as a shock among historians—as if it revealed that Brockway wasn't really a reformer, as he claimed to be. What it reveals, instead, is simply the self-righteousness common among reformers. Having learned that Brockway had personally delivered all 19,497 blows received by inmate offenders at Elmira between 1888 and 1893, an investigative committee wondered whether "any human being could inflict upon others such severe punishment, so constantly and in such amounts, without being absolutely brutalized thereby and losing all sympathy with human suffering."[4] Brockway's answer was Yes. He didn't think he had been brutalized, and perhaps he was right. He devoutly believed his own propaganda and did his best to embody the icon of stern but just authority that he was creating.

Brockway can be charged with confusing convicts with objects—objects to be disciplined, objects to be reformed, objects to be numbered and graded. But he cannot be charged with confusing convicts with himself, as other reformers have done, thus producing further confusions about the relationship between image and reality, prison art and prison life.

The best example may be Thomas Mott Osborne (1859–1926),

a complex person to whom almost everything appeared very simple, and the most famous of a long line of prison officials who thought they were duty-bound to upset the institutions they were hired to govern. Osborne was a former businessman who invested himself in reform movements, taking a particular interest in the affairs of the penitentiary at Auburn, New York, his hometown. In 1914 he received a surprise appointment as warden of Sing Sing. There he established the Mutual Welfare League, a scheme of convict self-government that gave inmates the right to elect their own leaders, supervise their own work, and judge their own disciplinary cases—all, of course, under the benevolent supervision of Thomas Mott Osborne. This would make Sing Sing less distant from the customs of the normal world and prepare prisoners for the lives they would lead when they returned to it.

The experiment was interesting, but how did Osborne know what was best for his subjects? As might be said of any prison warden, there were plenty of things he didn't know. A convict friend testified that in many ways "Mr. Osborne was hoodwinked and deluded by the men he trusted."[5] The knowledge he most relied on came from his own experience as an "inmate." In 1913 he had arranged for himself to be incarcerated for a week at Auburn, in order to learn the truth about prison life. Again, it was an interesting experiment, although it was severely compromised by the fact that before his imprisonment he assembled the convicts and gave a speech in which he explained what was going to happen. He dressed in as "Tom Brown," inmate number 33,333x, but he was always plainly Thomas Mott Osborne. The warden delivered the daily newspaper to his cell and conducted a tour for reporters who wanted to observe the new convict at work. Nevertheless, Osborne spent the rest of his life advertising his role as "convict" in every possible way—one of which was having his portrait painted in his inmate uniform.[6]

Beneath Osborne's many layers of unconscious phoniness, the prisoners at Sing Sing recognized a basic sincerity and a real, though strange, power of leadership. State political officials didn't perceive the same qualities. Their exact reasons remain unclear, but they lost no time launching a campaign against him. Although many charges were brought, the principal allegation was that he had sex with his prisoners. The specific claims were probably false, but his close relations with innumerable young inmates, who called him "Tom" and "pal" and "Dad," gave ample reason for suspicion. His displays of authenticity and sincerity looked too much like camouflage for something more vital. He was indicted for neglect of duty, perjury, and "various unlawful and unnatural acts."[7] The accusations alone would have sunk almost anybody else; but intellectuals, clergymen, and wealthy people rallied to his side, he beat the charges in court, and he returned in triumph to Sing Sing—only to resign three months later. His active career at the prison had lasted only about sixteen months.

Afterward, Osborne served for three years as warden of the

naval prison at Portsmouth, New Hampshire. He began by being voluntarily incarcerated (yet again); then he started another experiment in inmate self-government. This came to naught under the succeeding administration, while the experiment at Sing Sing (and a similar, earlier experiment at Auburn) degenerated into the means by which con bosses acquired corrupt power. It is possible that Osborne obscurely realized that whatever success he had in running a prison resulted primarily from the shock of his personality, the unusual lengths to which he would go in interesting inmates in his projects. But the shock wore off. Three years after Osborne's departure from Sing Sing, Lawes discovered "the same accumulation of dirt and filth" that he had noticed on a visit to the prison before Osborne took office.[8]

Osborne, like Brockway, was hopelessly self-righteous and sure of himself. Unlike Brockway, he intensely enjoyed the sensation of being simultaneously inside and outside normal society. His greatest pleasure was to go about in disguises that even his friends could not penetrate. When he collapsed and died on the streets of Auburn, he was garbed in a grotesque theatrical costume, in which he intended to view his son's performance in a play. It's no surprise that one of his last projects was a movie, modestly entitled "The Right Way," designed to demonstrate the reality of his prison reforms through the medium of dramatic art. At Sing Sing he had made a publicity film of "the Tom Brown story." And certainly, it was by acting well his part that he had convinced himself, and many of the inmates of Sing Sing, that he was actually on the Inside—actually, somehow, one of them.

The art of the Big House was, as usual, the art of transformation. By playing an inmate, Osborne had taken the obscure businessman who was himself and had turned him into Something, even if the Something was only Convict Tom Brown. The effect of his performance at Sing Sing was not to make the prison part of the normal world; it was only, and briefly, to make it a more complete work of art—a place of confinement that was also a symbol of spiritual renewal, a free republic operated by a self-admiring despot, proclaiming itself an image of authentic human relationships.

Osborne's transformation of himself into an inmate established something of a tradition among reformers. In 1998 the television journalist Ted Koppel had himself "incarcerated" in a Texas prison, as part of a series of reports on "crime and punishment" in the United States.[9] Everyone knew who Koppel was, just as everyone had known who Osborne was. Possibly the same cannot be said of the media critic of the *Washington Post* who in 1971 became inmate number 50061 in Pennsylvania's Huntingdon State Correctional Institution, spent six days there, and wrote a book about it. Allegedly, nobody on the Inside knew the truth, only the state officials who arranged the affair. In 1937 Hans Reimer, a sociologist, spent three months in the Kansas state pen without anyone present knowing who he was—a difficult accomplishment. But none of these adventures seems to have produced any insights that could not have been attained by reading books or consulting common sense.[10]

One curious fruit of the Osborne tradition of reform was the career of Tom Murton (1928–90), a college professor who in the late 1960s was appointed superintendent of the Tucker unit of the Arkansas state prison system. Like Osborne, Murton attempted revolutionary changes, including the establishment of an elected inmate council; like Osborne, he left his job after a brief but memorable time in office (thirteen months, compared with Osborne's sixteen). But Murton didn't quit; he was fired, by the reformist governor who had appointed him—a governor who had rapidly become disgusted by what he considered Murton's greed for publicity.

The publicity continued in *Brubaker,* the film starring Robert Redford and based on Murton's recollections of his gallant failure. Although the movie was evidently intended as a commentary on prison conditions in general, it had very little connection to any Big House. Tucker housed fewer than three hundred inmates, and there had never been any attempt to make it a serious, self-sufficient prison world. Inmates and civilians wandered into and out of the restricted area, the guards were armed convicts, and the only meaningful deterrent to violence or escape was the possibility of being whipped or shot. The purpose of the film, however, was not to study the special characteristics of penology in Arkansas; it was to dramatize the horrors of prison life in

America. Even the convict uniforms one sees in the movie aren't the Arkansas white cotton pullovers; they're something like typical northern blues.

Both the movie and Murton's book, *Accomplices to the Crime* (1969), urge the traditional reformist idea that prisons are brutal despotisms that can be redeemed only by their transformation into humanitarian despotisms. Murton and the filmmakers share Osborne's and Brockway's confidence in the ability of the Man in Charge to create a better world, if only he is left alone to do it— a reformist application of the Big House ideal of prison as a separate and total environment, under total control. Murton's book echoes the concept we've encountered before, in propaganda written on behalf of Stateville: the notion that a well-run prison is a "welfare state," where people's needs are met more efficiently than they are on the Outside. The problem, from Murton's point of view, is that the social system isn't yet complete: we (not simply the inmates at Tucker) are all "inmates of our culture," prisoners of institutions in which we are supposed to be "cared for" but, sadly, are not.[11]

Murton assumed that his own dramatic performance as a prison official was crucial in creating a just society, and he rebelled when other people tried to hog the spotlight. One of them was an aide to the governor who pretended to be an inmate in order to investigate the realities of prison life. To Murton, this was mere naïveté.[12] So it's amusing to see that in *Brubaker*, for which Murton served as technical adviser, Redford himself follows Osborne's example and poses as an inmate, using this bit of theater to discover the truth about the prison where he is going to act the part of godlike warden. The temptation was apparently irresistible. What would prison be without exciting transformations of identity?

Another person whom Osborne would have recognized as one of his descendants was Vernon Fox (1916–2001), the sociologist who played an important role in the riot at Jackson in 1952. Fox is in some ways an appealing personality. As a teenager, he had lived in a "commonwealth" for wayward and neglected boys. If life imitates art, as Oscar Wilde suggested, Fox was the real-life version of the reformist doctor in *Boys' Reformatory* (a prison picture of 1939), who is said to have spent two years in an institution for youth before beginning his role as Big House guardian and guru.

Fox was hired at Jackson as a deputy warden in charge of counseling and "individual treatment." He denied any intention of trying to take over the prison, but he worked steadily to aggrandize his side of the business. His colleagues in the "custodial" branch viewed him in roughly the same way in which the bad guys in a prison film always view the new, reformist officer. It wasn't a pleasant relationship, but its artistic precedents made it reassuringly predictable.[13]

Fox's great opportunity to reform Jackson arrived at the moment when the revolt in the segregation block became a riot that engulfed the rest of the penitentiary. Observing that other staff members were afraid to walk through the yard to talk with the rebels, Fox did so, making himself the de facto leader of the state's attempt to retake the institution. True to Jackson's slap-happy style of management, the warden allowed unlimited media access to the Inside, right from the start of the riot. The insurrection received more intimate coverage than any previous event in prison history, and Fox (who was a young, good-looking, well-spoken man) briefly became a hero, a glamorous precursor to Brubaker. His strategy was to get the inmates to make a list of demands, to which the governor of the state could then agree. His tactic was to create the list himself, ensuring that it would incorporate the reforms he wanted. Osborne had done the same thing, arranging for inmates to put his reform suggestions into petitions addressed to him.[14]

Fox's plan succeeded. But to make sure that the inmates kept their side of the agreement and stopped the riot, he went on prison radio and congratulated their leaders—whom he privately regarded as psychotics—on their "good faith" and the "service" they had provided to the cause of prison reform. He said that they had "won." He hailed their chief as a "natural leader."[15] It was then he discovered that there are limits to the ability of the Big House to incorporate images of progress. It can welcome the image of the reformer as hero; it can even welcome the image of the inmate as countercultural hero (*Jailhouse Rock*, *Shawshank Redemption*, *Escape from Alcatraz* [1979]); it cannot—except as perceived by extreme advocates of social reform—incorporate the image of the inmate as master of the institution. When inmates are acknowledged as leaders of the Big House, the Big House loses its integrity as an icon. And where prisons are concerned, public opinion is informed by the Big House icon; life, again, imitates art. So Fox's drama of reform turned into a drama of expulsion. A wave of anger swept the state, and he was fired from his job. Fox left prison management, became a college professor, and was never heard of again, except by academic experts.

The Riot (1966), one of the best-written and most authentic of Big House novels (its author, Frank Elli, was serving time in Minnesota when he wrote it), contains a cruel satire of a young prison psychologist who manages to put himself in charge of both the administration and the rioting convicts. Unlike everyone else in the book, this reformer always gives "the appearance of a man who had enjoyed a restful night's sleep."[16] Vernon Fox can't be accused of that. At worst, he can be accused of doing what the Big House encourages reformers to do—see it as a theater, and themselves as directors, expressing their sincerity by staging a performance. If he had come a few years later in institutional history, he might have become the protagonist of a major motion picture—another Brubaker.

Until the 1960s, however, the best way for a prison administrator to achieve public applause was to combine humanitarian spirit with unquestioned executive authority (which Fox, unfortunately, turned out not to have). The most propitious of all eras was the 1930s and 1940s, the heroic age of big government, when reform and authority derived legitimacy from each other as much as they ever have in American history. During this period, the Big House received overwhelmingly favorable treatment in the popular press and generally respectful treatment in film. It was the era of the great, publicity-making wardens: Joseph Ragen of Stateville, Clinton Duffy of San Quentin, and Lewis Lawes of Sing Sing, each one playing Franklin D. Roosevelt in his own sovereign republic. They wrote books, they were worshiped by journalists, they made warm friends with the camera.

When Lawes (1883–1947) became Osborne's successor at Sing Sing, he found that the place had returned to its ordinary spiritual and physical squalor, a condition that revealed either the futility of Osborne's reforms or the evil of not continuing them. Lawes institutionalized Osborne's ideas—such as the Mutual Welfare League—so artfully that it was difficult to tell whether the inmates had a say about anything or not. It was clear that he worked to improve the physical conditions of their lives, and also that he was an avid publicizer of his own accomplishments, real or imaginary. He wrote six books about himself and his views on punishment. There were also four movies "based" on his work; a magazine, *Prison Life Stories;* two lucrative series of radio programs; and many speaking tours and engagements. He appeared on the cover of *Time.* He was even willing, for the benefit of charity, to put on a striped suit and have himself photographed as a convict.[17]

Despite his many virtues as a prison reformer and administrator, Joseph Ragen was also guilty of enormous crimes in the field of public relations. He commissioned a journalist to sing his praises at the length of eighty thousand words.[18] He published his own 939-page history and description of Stateville, a book that reproduces his bureaucratic forms and orders as if they were improved editions of the Mosaic law.[19] He wrote another book, which mercifully remains in manuscript. In it, fictional convicts talk by the hour about life in Stateville, with particular attention to the warden's almost miraculous power and wisdom.[20] But the true source of Ragen's success as a self-publicizer was his ability to show reporters and visitors a prison that looked exactly like what they thought a prison should look like—massive, confident, rigorously disciplined, the Big House in its virtually Platonic form.

Public tours and visits constituted a major front in the fight for publicity. Osborne showed real talent at shanghaiing wealthy or otherwise influential people into visiting his prison—where, says his admiring biographer, they "marveled at the thing Sing Sing had become."[21] Lawes provided tours for up to three thousand civilians a day. When Clinton Duffy (1898–1982) arrived at San Quentin in 1940, he found tourists distressingly few. So he began inviting "groups of carefully selected civilians into the big house," where they received "carefully guided tours." The stated purpose was to help inmates remember what the outside world was like; the chief influence, however, was on journalists and their impressions of Duffy. He even convinced the people at *Life* that inmates "regard[ed] him more as friend than keeper."[22] For reformers, the Big House—their own official version of the Big

House—was a work of persuasive art: they persuaded opinion makers to persuade their audiences that the inmates had been persuaded by the warden. As you might expect, Duffy had movies made in his honor: *San Quentin* (1946) and *Duffy of San Quentin* (1954), advertised as "the big story of Warden Duffy, who made a model prison of the world's toughest jail."[23]

This sort of thing undoubtedly helped to keep prison budgets up. "Models" or not, San Quentin, Sing Sing, and Stateville appeared to be progressive and assertive institutions, appropriate to an era of activist government with big plans for reshaping society. Ragen's penitentiary represented itself not only as a "welfare state" whose inhabitants were "never in doubt about where their next meal [was] coming from" but also as an "empire," "a complete social and economic system," and a "modern factory" that was perfectly capable of turning a profit, if only competing interests would allow it to do so.[24] Stateville seemed to exemplify everything that was efficient and effective in the modern world—strong leadership, social planning, high ideals associated with practical know-how. It was a small-scale version of New Deal America.

Like a number of the other important wardens of his time, the emperor of Stateville had ambitious ideas of social reform: the immediate razing of all slums, state superintendency of the right to marry and produce children, and "the one-year-to-life sentence for *all* crimes." This last proposal, based on principles going back to Brockway, and before, would give prison officials total power over every convict's existence. Even a minor offense would result in a lifetime behind bars, unless the culprit got a favorable report from his keepers. But Ragen was not overly concerned with the individual. The premise on which he ran Stateville was the premise on which, he believed, society itself should be run: "More than any other single principle, civilization is based on the desire for the 'greatest good for the greatest number.' If personal propensities conflict with the trend of society as a whole, then personal propensities must be subordinated. This is not merely a hypothesis; it is a proven proposition, and any man with the capacity for rationalization will admit that the proof is logical."[25]

Lawes had his own proposals, not dissimilar to those of Ragen, about razing slums and building "model tenements."[26] He also entertained more advanced speculations. He thought that if everyone who committed a serious crime was caught and sent to jail, there would be nine times more convicts than there were when he wrote. Reflecting (not very insightfully) on the increase in prison commitments during Prohibition, he suggested that in three generations, one of three males between the ages of fifteen and sixty would be a convict. He toyed with the idea that if crime could be eradicated by the death penalty, "society could afford" to execute everyone in prison. When you think of it, he said, "more than ten times that number of lives were sacrificed" in World War I. But he didn't believe the death penalty would work. In fact, he opposed the death penalty, because the "inequality" and "infrequency" of its application, and the emotions it aroused, tended "to weaken our entire structure of social control." What would work, he believed, was a gargantuan effort to "provid[e] for each and every individual an equality of opportunity."[27]

The assumption was that crime results from environment, and environment can be closely controlled and engineered—obviously by people like Lawes, who knew how to run a controlled institution. Although Lawes believed that convicts "are not very different from the rest of us," this was not an idea he applied to himself. He was very disappointed that he and his family had to live in Sing Sing, "as securely locked within the walls as any of the prisoners." For himself, he wanted "privacy."[28] It was only "the rest of us" whom he was tempted to confuse with convicts.

Like Ragen, Lawes advocated the indeterminate sentence, with a vengeance: "A person sent to prison ought to be committed until reformed or until death."[29] This was a from-now-to-the-grave welfare policy if ever there was one, and it is surprising that more concern was not shown for its probable results. The effects of indeterminate sentences on convict morale have already been mentioned; they were bad even when sentences didn't end with "until death." The effects on administrative morale were not much better. The problem was one that naturally arises in a welfare state: the authorities who are commissioned to plan other people's lives can never seem to get enough reliable information to justify their decisions. When the indeterminate sentence was seriously tried, as it was by Governor Earl Warren's administration in California in the 1940s, it involved psychosocial "treatment," administered in "group counseling" sessions, and a board of experts that regularly reviewed each convict to see whether the disease of criminality had been sufficiently controlled to allow him to be released. But the information that the experts had at their disposal consisted mainly of records of the convict's desire to impress the authorities by "participating" in "programs."[30] To put the problem another way: a Big House that was big enough to encompass the convict's entire world, an institution that really tried not simply to confine him securely, as at Ragen's Stateville, but also to educate, reform, "treat," "socialize," and in every other respect look after his well-being, was a Big House that could not be adequately monitored and controlled. This is an idea we've met before, in other contexts—an idea that is easy to understand, but that few reformers, even Ragen, seemed able to assimilate.

And then, in the 1960s, the Big House crashed.

NINE

Prisons You Can't Tear Down

"Haven't you seen any prison movies?" That's what the hero of *Let's Go to Prison* says to a new fish who makes the mistake of giving evidence against a fellow convict. Prison movies always caution against that kind of thing, and their advice is good, up to a point. But any convict who took popular culture as a guide to the Big House would be in trouble. Popular culture has never concerned itself with the complexities of prison life.

In the mid-twentieth century, however, popular culture was surprisingly perceptive about the future of prisons. It foreshadowed what was going to happen to the Big House—partly by mirroring attitudes about prison that were held by people of influence, attitudes that were gradually becoming hostile; and partly just by representing prison as artistic considerations suggested.

The midcentury antagonism toward custom and authority among the creators of popular attitudes—writers, filmmakers, social commentators—did not spare the penal system. Prisons lost their screen of favorable publicity and became vulnerable to deconstructive criticism. But the storytelling media had their own imperatives. They always do. Movies, books, and television programs need to tell *good* stories, stories that *go* someplace, and in this regard prison stories have inherent limitations. Prisons aren't people, they're situations; they can't carry a plot on their own. The three most obvious ways of creating a story about prisons are by showing people (1) rebelling against them, (2) trying to get out of them, and (3) trying to change them. In all three cases, prison becomes the antagonist.

This tendency was already apparent in the nineteenth century, when many print runs were devoted to stories about prisoners who escaped confinement by reforming themselves, and about prison officials and prison missionaries who tried to help them do so. Such stories often reflected poorly on prison itself, because the personal reform they depicted usually happened more in spite of prison than because of it. In the late nineteenth and early twentieth centuries many books of another kind appeared, directed at a lowest-common-denominator popular audience— books in which convicts or ex-convicts told sensational stories about the "hell" of life in one prison or another.[1] If these works had any effect, it was to demonstrate the need for prison reform, especially in backward parts of the country (though doubtless they also served to advertise prison as a realm of raw excitements and interesting cruelties).

When motion pictures arrived in the twentieth century, they needed other kinds of material. Until the 1960s few prison movies were unremittingly raw or sensational; the same sanitizing process that operated with sex operated with prisons. And personal reform could hardly be sustained as a film's basic plot: reform takes too long, if it's represented realistically, and it offers small potential for dramatic action. While convicts, especially nice young convicts, are frequently reformed in mid-twentieth-century pictures, their stories are inconsequential compared with the prison setting.

The important question is what the movies did with that setting. Big House films of the 1930s and 1940s, when large numbers of these films were produced, usually regarded the institution as a social necessity: its existence was unfortunate, but its essential functions were useful and respectable. Because of the storytelling necessity, however, most of these films were about people who rebelled against, attempted to escape from, or attempted to reform the prisons they lived or worked in. This is a significant phenomenon in a society that devoted considerable amounts of attention, money, and even admiration to its prisons. Cinematic versions of the Big House often portrayed wardens or guards as despots, or as dull pieces of custodial hardware, while inmates were portrayed as the luckless subjects of such people, innocent either by comparison or by default.

Within These Walls (1945), is the story of a warden (Thomas Mitchell) whose rebellious son commits a crime and is sentenced to the same prison that his father runs: "I'm not his son anymore; I'm just a number." Even in this peculiar case, the focus is on the authoritarianism of the warden, not the guilt or folly of the prisoner. Only after his son is killed in an escape attempt does the warden repent of his cold devotion to discipline. It's a common story in prison films: the Big House won't reform unless there's a radical change of personnel—although usually the change is the replacement of sadistic officers with reformist ones, not the conversion of the warden himself. Yet, everything considered, *Within These Walls* is favorable to the Big House as an institution. "We want to help you," the reformed warden says to a newly admitted convict at the end of the film. "We want to do everything we can to make you a useful citizen." And there's no reason to believe that the statement is supposed to be viewed critically. There is still nothing essentially wrong with the Big House.

That generalization doesn't hold for cinematic prisons of the 1950s and beyond. In the older movies, convicts tend to be picturesque mugs or young leading men who wind up in jail for one reason or another and want to get out of it. The story is about whether they succeed. But as the twentieth century wears on, individual convicts become more admirable and more interesting; their crimes, if any, matter even less than crimes mattered before; and prison is no longer taken seriously as a socially sanctioned institution.

The protagonist of *The Shawshank Redemption* has been sentenced to life for a pair of murders he didn't commit; his sidekick is a stir-wise con who actually is a murderer. But so what? Compared with the fanatically cruel and corrupt prison guards and officials, both men are saints. The hero of *Cool Hand Luke* (1967) —a film about a southern prison barracks that is, like *Brubaker,* apparently meant to have a wider reference to American society— has been incarcerated for the innocuous crime of getting drunk and vandalizing parking meters. His sidekick is evidently in prison for some more serious offense, which the movie cares nothing about. It draws no moral contrast between the venial and the mortal sinner. The important thing is the contrast between the toughness and sensitivity of the convicts and the vile oppressiveness of their captors.

During the era of the great wardens, the Big House could still be presented as an imposing social institution, the massive object of the camera's love. True, men wanted to escape from it, yet the interest usually lay in the intensity of their struggle, not in the rightness of their cause. Think of the mess hall scene in *White Heat* (1949). In a room that is filmed to appear gigantic, long rows of identically uniformed convicts are metallically chewing their food. Suddenly one man (Cody Jarrett, played by James Cagney), a psychopath, leaps up and makes a hopeless dash for freedom: "Lemme out! I wanta get outta here!" At that point, no one in the audience cares whether he's a criminal or not (although he is, and one of the worst); what people appreciate is the kind of drama that only a Big House can stage. This is true even about such sentimentalized, do-good pictures as *20,000 Years in Sing Sing*. The prison makes the drama.

But attitudes were changing. Consider a pair of prison films, each starring Burt Lancaster and each prophetic of bad days coming for the Big House in the court of public esteem. In the first, *Brute Force* (1947), the intelligent, sadistic, manifestly homosexual captain of Westgate Penitentiary (Hume Cronyn), his office adorned with pictures of muscly male nudes, tortures prisoners while listening to recordings of *Tannhäuser*. When Lancaster, a heroic convict, leads an attack on this latter-day Elam Lynds, the film seems unconscious of the fact that the tactics of the rebels are almost as sadistic as those of their adversary. The revolt is crowned with symbolic success: moments before his own Christlike death, Lancaster manages to kill the captain by heaving him from the top of a guard tower. This is, perhaps, an odd way for a Christ figure to perform, but it's the best that can be done in a Big House rendered as an existential hell. The film ends with a statement by the prison doctor: "Nobody ever really escapes!" The implication of this poetic hyperbole is that prison, as a totalitarian institution, is a model of modern American life, which is the only thing inclusive enough to justify the remark. If so, it's one more tribute to the symbolic importance of the Big House, but it's clearly not a respectful assessment of either the Big House or the country that produced it.

The attack on the Big House, and anything it might imply

about American institutions, continues in the second Lancaster film, *Birdman of Alcatraz* (1962). Here Lancaster plays Robert Stroud (1890–1963), a man who committed a murder in Alaska Territory in 1909, was sentenced to federal prison, tried to kill a fellow convict in 1911, then succeeded in killing a guard at Leavenworth in 1916.[2] For understandable reasons, the prison service segregated Stroud from the general population. Nevertheless, like many other inmates of the time, he was allowed to keep pet birds in his cell, and he made himself an expert on bird diseases. He published articles and books, dispensed veterinary advice (which was often wrong), and ran a large mail-order business in birds and bird medicine. Prison authorities broke down a wall and gave him a double cell so that he could house the hundreds of birds that flew about him, befouling his quarters and himself. He was proudly exhibited to visitors. At tremendous cost in time and labor, Leavenworth processed his shipments of birds and his immense correspondence. But when America entered World War II and there was a shortage of manpower to staff the prisons, Stroud was moved to Alcatraz, where he could be segregated with less maintenance. His bird business ended, yet his fame was just beginning.

In 1955 a man named Thomas E. Gaddis, who had become convinced that Stroud was a heroic victim of the prison bureaucracy, published a book to that effect. *Birdman of Alcatraz* became a best-seller and convinced even some penologists that Stroud "was constantly thwarted by the administration."[3] Lancaster's movie followed. It omitted the fact that its protagonist was a repulsive human being—grossly self-centered, tyrannical, conscienceless, and addicted to writing pederastic fiction. With some truth and much invention, it made Stroud into an icon within an icon: an intransigent individualist maintaining his integrity of self amid the fearful regimentation of the Big House. The filmmakers clearly had no intention of exploring any more complex features of prison life, such as the ability of eccentric individuals to turn a presumably total environment to their own advantage.

As a prisoner, Stroud succeeded—by wheedling, hectoring, and just being the obnoxious person he was—in creating a life for himself that he was reluctant to surrender merely to be paroled. Death came at the medical facility at Springfield, Missouri, a few months after Alcatraz closed. Although Stroud brought Alcatraz a lot of bad publicity, he himself had advocated that all convicts be sent to maximum security institutions. He had even offered to help the government design the right kind of prisons to house them.[4] There is little doubt that he understood the Big House a great deal better than the people who tried to extricate him from it. The *Birdman* stories allegedly illustrated the penitentiary's skill at torturing its inmates. What they actually showed was one prisoner's capacity to transform prison into the sole offender.

By now, the climate of elite opinion, once favorable to the Big House (supposing that it was reasonably well run), was becoming distinctly unfavorable. Gone were the days when the big national magazines were happy to discover that a warden "welcomes prisoners' problems, will always listen," or noted with complacency that "inmates here must forget the meaning of privacy and individuality."[5] During the 1950s and 1960s, the power of the modern state was coming under increasingly heavy fire from both left and right. Prisons made an inevitable target.

Some Big House experts condemned their very existence. In 1954 the producers of NBC's nine-hour investigative report on prisons, two exceptionally acute and well-informed investigators, accepted as proven fact the idea that "fear of punishment does not deter crime."[6] During the same year, the journalist and politician John Bartlow Martin, whose reports on prisons have often been cited here, published a book entitled *Break Down the Walls*. Martin, a speechwriter for Adlai Stevenson, described prison as "the enemy of society" and proposed the establishment of a vast research organization to unearth the causes of crime. "Once we have discovered what makes men criminal," he argued, deploying a plausible non sequitur, "we shall know how to rehabilitate them." Prisons could then be replaced with truly therapeutic institutions.[7]

A different form of abolitionism manifested itself in the radical movements of the 1960s. Its motivating idea was that prisons really do work, but to the wrong ends: they are the means by which a racist and plutocratic society oppresses the working class. Although the radicals were unconscious of the precedent, they agreed with admirers of the Big House in regarding it as a microcosm of America—in the old expression, "just like a large city." The difference was that they saw it not as an American "welfare state" but as a revelation of American "fascism." As a former participant in the radical prison reform movement has observed, "the shock [!] of discovering San Quentin to be a totalitarian state" was taken as "proof that America itself was one."[8]

The federal government never suffered that kind of shock, but it was already working to give "rehabilitation" a much higher priority than "punishment." It led the way in constructing smaller institutions with lighter security—a different concept from that of the Big House, where the levels of security that were needed for the most dangerous inmates usually set the levels for everyone else. Robert Barnes, senior architect for the federal Bureau of Prisons, boasted that in the 1938–40 period the Bureau had constructed only "about fifteen million dollars' worth of prison buildings and probably used only about $500 worth of tool-proof steel."[9] California took an additional step. It created the "prison without walls," busing in thirty-four inmates who didn't require the high security of San Quentin.

Liberal views of prison were strengthened, not weakened, by the big wave of riots in the early 1950s at Jackson and other institutions.[10] An apt symbol of the emerging liberal consensus is *Riot in Cell Block 11* (1954), a film by Don Siegel, one of Hollywood's better directors. The movie opens with newsreel scenes from the riots of 1952. Some of the prisons are mislabeled, but accuracy is not the point: this is a polemic. The newsreel is followed by an interview, in which a reformist expert blames riots on "short-sighted neglect" of prisons—a neglect "amounting to almost criminal negligence"—by public officials and the public itself. Threatening language is used about riots yet to come. Then the fictional story begins. It's a reenactment of the crisis at Jackson. An inmate in the segregation unit waylays an incompetent guard, he releases other inmates from their cells, the unit is trashed, and so on. The guards are portrayed, by and large, as callous about the sufferings of their prisoners, who are depicted in various sympathetic postures. Nevertheless, when the riot breaks out, the guards are allowed to comment on the conditions of their own lives, and it is revealed that they are victims of the Big House too:

GUARD A: Well, here we go again [as if riots take place every day].

GUARD B: Yeah, and all for fifty bucks a week.

The warden and the state governor also converse, and we learn that conservative politicians are the source of the prison problem.

WARDEN: I warned you we were due for a riot. I've even got 'em sleeping in the corridors of Block 4.

GOVERNOR (who has an American flag prominently displayed on his desk): You're *always* talking about overcrowding, old plant, insufficient personnel.

165

In other words, so what? Let the guards and convicts suffer: that's the American way.

Reciting typical prison-reform talking points, the warden tells the press, "We've got all kinds here—good and bad, just like on the outside." And although the riot is immediately taken over by "unbalanced" inmates, modeled closely on the crazies at Jackson, their aim from the start is reform. The ostensibly insane leader of the insurrection summons the press and does an able job extending the warden's arguments on this topic. Reacting to the inmates' proposals, the state prison commissioner asks the warden, "Are you sure you didn't write these demands yourself?" The warden tells the press, "Most of them have been my demands for a long time." He's responding in the tradition of Osborne and Fox, who were happy to provide their own demands for the inmates to reproduce.

At riot's end, the demands are accepted, and an obliging newspaperman suggests that "congratulations are in order." The warden chimes in and says that "the inmates won" the riots of 1952. It's straight out of Fox's radio speech. The big difference is that Fox was fired at Jackson, but *Cell Block 11* was made at Folsom, with the official cooperation of the authorities, who were apparently in sympathy with its demands. They may have appreciated the celluloid warden's outraged complaint: "The legislature's never given me the money I need."

In the movie, the politicians renege on their agreement, thus proving the filmmakers' point about public neglect of prison reform. Yet real politicians were getting the message. Those who were worried about prisons in their states began paying guards better and training them more professionally. Funds were allocated to take inmates out of the Big House and put them into new systems of camps and reformatories with lower security, inspired by the federal classification system. And bigger changes were in store. Until the 1960s, courts had taken a largely hands-off attitude toward prisons. Thereafter, they dramatically extended their concern with inmate rights, contesting custodial power over institutions that had formerly been treated as separate worlds, isolated from judicial interference. On the Inside, the new emphasis on a professionalized staff meant that old-line managers who had grown up in prison work were being replaced by a new crowd of college graduates, to whom the Big House often seemed an alien and archaic institution. Many of them had been trained in social work and related disciplines and were eager to apply theories of society that were more appropriate to the Outside than to the Inside. Their approach led even reformist liberals to complain that "social workers . . . are often zealots."[11] In 1970 one of Joseph Ragen's successors as warden of Stateville, a former graduate student in sociology, astonished the prison population by announcing that he had come to "serve" the inmates.[12] Such declarations were significant for what they said about the weakness of the administration's self-confidence. To an intelligent convict, they could only mean "We intend to let you have as much power as you are able to seize."

Politics was returning to the Big House. The issue wasn't which political party had won the last election and could therefore appoint the staff. Partisan politics no longer figured that strongly. The issue now was the politics of ethnicity. The presence of large numbers of African American prisoners convinced many people on the left that the vanguard of the civil rights movement was "the prison movement"—radical agitation for prison reform. In 1971, the riot occurred at Attica—a large, soulless institution in western New York, built to fulfill the most modern standards of the 1930s. Prison activists turned the riot into a "rebellion" and a political cause for "progressive" civilians. Once the Big House became an arena of political combat, it was obviously not a "world of its own," as the *Chicago Tribune* had pronounced it just a decade and a half before.[13]

This was bad enough for the Big House; but the massacre that attended the state's ill-planned suppression of the revolt at Attica said something even worse about the legitimacy of prison as a secure and stable institution, an object of civic pride. Earlier in 1971 California's prison system had earned its own bad publicity when George Jackson, an inmate, used a smuggled gun to release fellow "revolutionaries" in San Quentin's euphemistically named Adjustment Center. Hostages were taken and slaughtered, and Jackson was gunned down by a marksman guard. Six people died.[14]

At Attica less than one-seventh as many lives were lost as in the disaster at the Ohio Penitentiary in 1930, but reactions to such events were now very different. The official attitude to riots following the Ohio fire was that "prisoners could take their chances of going to a morgue or conducting themselves according to the rules." When two big riots occurred at Auburn in 1929, state troopers recaptured the prison, unembarrassed by any compunctions about loss of lives—their own, those of the convicts, or those of the convicts' hostages. No objections were made. Governor Roosevelt contemptuously rejected the idea that riots could not be prevented without fundamental changes in the prison system.[15] At that time, tough talk, along with some money to build a better Big House, satisfied the public. In the 1970s talk no longer sufficed, and there were no more Big Houses on the drafting boards. People of influence were learning to see convicts mainly as victims of social injustice, and prisons, especially big prisons, mainly as agents of political repression. According to this line of reasoning, the only way to reform the prison was to empower the inmates. Many radical critics of the Big House were already working inside it, to do just that.

By the end of the decade, discipline had collapsed in one prison after another, replaced by the authority of ethnically polarized inmate gangs. In some prisons, inmate "councils" attained power, but the results were not exactly what Thomas Mott Osborne had envisioned. At the Washington State Penitentiary, self-government ultimately meant that the prison was dominated by predatory "clubs" of bikers and lifers, with money and self-esteem supplied by drugs. In other places (such as Stateville), the administration forfeited its power to the convict representatives of black and Hispanic street gangs. As early as 1971, the warden of San Quentin complained to the press that armies of black "revolutionary" inmates were massing in his yard for drill. The "treatment staff" of his institution enabled convicts to operate radical political organizations, entertain radical orators, and bring in contraband literature. Volunteer tutors helped California inmates develop the Symbionese Liberation Army, the most famous "revolutionary cadre" of the 1970s.[16]

Interviewed about the innovations in the state of Washington, a sociologist got down to the basic issue. Regretting that the Big House was "so unnecessarily punitive," he suggested that prison should be "as much like life on the outside as possible."[17] Despite its genesis in Osborne's ideas about giving people on the inside civilian-like responsibilities, to fit them for life on the outside, it was still a remarkable conception—that people should be punished by being confined to the environments from which they came. Nothing could be farther from the Big House idea—or from any defensible, or comprehensible, goal of penology. Substantive ideas were being replaced by symbols and images, with little reference to experience or fact. The corrections official in charge of the Reform Movement in Washington State was guided by metaphors of prison officers as parents, doctors, teachers, and friends—anything but what they were. He thought that inmates would no longer see themselves as inmates if they were called "residents" and their prison was called "the program." Denouncing the process of turning "human beings" into "numbers," he proposed to change the system by introducing "rehabilitative services" that were "comprehensive . . . concerned with the total person." "Services" meant programs, elections, and meetings, meetings, meetings. Formerly, prisons transformed men by putting numbers on their backs; now men would be transformed by politics and euphemisms.[18]

To be fair, the unstated assumptions of such reform experiments were those of the Big House itself: that men can be transformed, either into numbers or into free and responsible citizens, by being processed into some comprehensive system of life; that prison officials possess the knowledge and power to manage such a system effectively; and that success depends to an important degree on the artful employment of symbols and rituals. Inmates couldn't escape from the new experiments any more than they could from the Big House; and in neither case was the outcome encouraging.

At first, and as usual, the media were on the side of the reformists. Then suddenly they discovered that prisons were actually coming to resemble the outside world, in its most sordid aspects. At the Washington State Penitentiary, *Life* reported, "Prisoners can do almost anything they want with their free time, including, for one group, riding motorcycles at high speed around the yard. Cells are decorated to their occupants' taste. There are no uniforms, and transvestites often wear blouses and mini-dresses as they mix with the other prisoners." Next to these comments appeared the photograph of "a young prisoner who is the private sexual property of an older, tougher convict." The youngster was shown relaxing in an elaborately furnished cell, casually displaying the black eye he got as "punishment for having sex with another prisoner."[19] The sexual secrets of the Big House were finally being exposed, for the benefit of every junior high school student whose library subscribed to *Life*, but the institution on display was no longer the Big House that had exhibited itself so proudly to earlier generations. It wasn't a work of art, even bad art. It was madness.

Once more, guards and officials were surrendering prison to the inmates. "The staff doesn't own one piece of ground in there, not an inch," said the warden at Washington. In penitentiaries throughout the country, violence soared, and living conditions increasingly resembled those in many third-world prisons, where everything is permitted but nothing works. The record at Washington was three murders during the 1960s, twenty-four during the 1970s.[20] Riots broke out at Stateville (1973) and in New Mexico (1980), West Virginia (1986), Washington itself (1979, 1980, 1981), and other places suffering from lax or incompetent administration. The outbreak at the New Mexico Penitentiary resulted in hideous inmate-on-inmate brutality. The riot at Stateville involved the capture of the largest cellblock and the homosexual rape of several guards.[21] By 1979 Stateville—where inmates had formerly snapped to attention as the warden walked the yard—had achieved, according to its own management, "a reputation as a violent, overcrowded, and inmate-controlled prison . . . dangerous, on the verge of chaos, and maintaining substandard living conditions."[22] "Substandard" meant that no-body's life was safe.

A prominent sociologist summarized the situation: "In con-temporary institutions [guards] have withdrawn to the walls, leaving inmates to intimidate, rape, maim, and kill each other with alarming frequency." He added the same personal comment that convicts and guards have often made: "If I had to do time . . . I would do my time in [an old-fashioned] Big House," not in a contemporary prison where "policing" had lost its prestige.[23]

As one might predict, Jackson illustrated what could go wrong with a prison. After the riot of 1952, it began to get serious about officers' pay and training; it even attained a more orderly and professional regime. Then, in the 1970s, it did what reformers had urged for a long time: it started breaking itself into smaller units, subprisons that presumably didn't require the single-minded devotion of a Joseph Ragen to administer. One side of the prison was divided from the rest and joined to a new set of living quarters, built outside the walls and circled by new fortifi-cations of razor wire—contrary to the advice of a warden who, two decades before, had sensibly observed that more enclosures demand more supervision.[24] In 1981 riots erupted in both sides of the institution, sparked, ironically, by the increasingly profes-sionalized officer staff, which staged a work protest against the administration's indulgence of the inmates.[25]

The riots were suppressed, but by the mid-1980s Jackson was chronically out of control. Inmates wore their own clothes, if they could afford them, reducing the distinction between "offenders" and "officers" to that between the stylishly and the stodgily dressed. Cells were left unlocked during the day, and inmates who cared about their possessions put their own padlocks on the bars. An academic book appeared, devoted solely to the economics of prostitution, drugs, burglary, and bribery in Jackson Prison. Guards had concluded, the author wrote, that control of prisoners was the administration's "last priority."[26] In 1975 a helicopter landed next to the license plate factory and made off with one of the inmates, flying past a guard tower that was staffed by a TV camera instead of a human being (so much for modern technology). Early in 1987 an inmate seized a woman officer, raped her, and beat her to death. Nine months later, a male officer was slain. These were thought to be the first two killings of guards in Jackson's history—because earlier killings had been forgotten. The brother of the second victim informed the governor of Michigan that the deaths were not surprising: prisoners had so "many freedoms and rights, and guards so little means of protection. My brother once said, 'The prisoners allow us to work here.'"[27]

At this point, it wasn't the repressive Big House that was under fire; it was the anti–Big House idea that the less discipline you apply, the better things will be. Observers noticed that significant riots tended to occur in prisons where there were few guards (West Virginia), inadequate structures of control (Attica, New

Mexico), or reformers who had conceded substantial power to inmates (Washington), which meant conceding it to the most cunning, violent, and demagogic members of the inmate population.[28] During the 1980s and 1990s the states responded forcefully to the problem of control. Across the nation, security was increased, discipline was tightened, and officers were trained in better means of managing prisoners. By 1990, the elite media were reporting that prison violence and disorder had been substantially reduced.[29]

This doesn't imply that the Big House had received public vindication. It hadn't. Like many other fixtures of American culture, the Big House had been permanently damaged by the combined effects of two competing political visions, each emanating from the 1960s. It had been swamped first by a tidal wave of left-liberalism, then by an opposing wave of conservatism. Liberals objected to the Big House itself; conservatives objected to its failure to operate as it ought to.

Lack of support for the Big House wasn't a matter of money. The American public, which was incomparably richer than it had been in the nineteenth century, was more willing than ever to spend money on incarceration. Crime rates started rising in the 1960s, and a few years later prison populations rose in response, after law and order became a leading conservative issue. In 1996 prisons received five times more people from the courts than they had in 1968.[30] A large percentage of these offenders had been sentenced for victimless crimes—mainly drug violations—

but any inspection of inmate records will indicate that many of the same people had also committed less subjective offenses. The collapse of penal discipline strengthened the conservative argument for punishment, as contrasted with rehabilitation, which apparently didn't work. Many liberal analysts no longer trusted the concept, either; and popular journalism now despaired of it.[31] Convict ranks were swelled by the mass release of mental patients from state hospitals—a combined effect of liberal agitation for human rights and conservative agitation against social welfare expenditures. So inmates of one set of institutions became inmates of another. In the 1980s and 1990s America pursued the largest prison building program in its history. New institutions were founded, older institutions acquired new high-security units, and (eventually) a renewed emphasis was placed on discipline for convicts as well as staff.

But the money didn't go to rebuild the Big House on its old foundations. Funds were channeled by professional penologists (who favored less populous institutions) and professional politicians (who favored widely distributed rewards for local voters) into a myriad of smaller prisons, scattered across rural areas where government jobs were appreciated.

Today, Georgia has forty-seven state penal institutions, Oklahoma twenty-seven, Ohio thirty-two, Michigan fifty-one. Most of these institutions aren't just small; they're shy. If they aren't mere "camps" lurking at the ends of obscure country roads, they are earth-colored "facilities" hiding behind grass-covered "berms." Many resemble warehouses in an industrial park. The contemporary inmate "housing unit" isn't a six-story cellblock with hundreds of convicts marching along the galleries. It's a two-level "pod" with thirty solid-doored cells on each level and a "day room" at the center, where a guard can watch the prisoners while they watch TV. In some places, food is brought to the pod from a remote source—like pizza.

To deal with the most violent convicts, many states have constructed "supermax" prisons or prison units. Here offenders spend virtually every hour of every day immured in cells where even the beds are concrete. Instead of bars, these cells have solid steel doors, with little windows through which guards can occasionally peer, and little "ports" through which inmates can thrust their arms to be cuffed when they are taken out for brief periods of solitary exercise. This isn't the "hole" that we see in movies, nor is it the site of constant surveillance about which Bentham, Foucault, and the builders of Stateville fantasized.[32] It's an institution that attempts to eliminate the problems of order, discipline, and surveillance itself by the simple expedient of immobilizing the convicts in concrete caverns. And to a large extent, it succeeds in doing that, allowing other penal institutions to maintain lower levels of security for the less difficult inmates they house.

The world of the new American prison was born, and it wasn't simply the Big House reborn. It was a complexly negotiated settlement between the conservative concern for order and the liberal (and court-mandated) concern for convicts' rights and material well-being. The result is today's professionalized prison: smallish, rule-bound, bureaucratic, insistently "fair," though often in a niggling, cover-your-ass way; a place where rules are enforced with a ponderous rationality that was largely absent from the Big House. Though it lacks the surly grandeur of the Big House, it is usually a cleaner, more orderly, and more humane institution, staffed by officers who are many times more competent and responsible than was the ordinary Big House crew.

Still, none of today's prisons, with the exception of costly supermax units, achieves the degree of control over convict life that Warden Ragen achieved at Stateville. The yards and corridors of too many prisons are dominated by racial gangs—black, Hispanic, "Aryan." Too many convicts are housed in low-security dorms stacked three-high with bunks, wastelands in which a few predators can make life hell for everyone else. These structures satisfy liberals' traditional demand for less restraint and conservatives' traditional demand for less spending on amenities (dormitories cost a small fraction of what cellblocks cost). But both convicts and officers uniformly report that they would rather serve a sentence in a single-man cell in an old-time cellhouse than in any such modern substitute.

The essential problems of living in prison remain, and so do the problems of designing prisons that maintain their distance from the outside world, so that they can function as prisons. Many traditional solutions to these problems are still, perhaps inevitably, in use: the architecture of total enclosure; the formalized routine; the procedures of initiation, designed to transform persons into compliant objects; the physical array of locks and bars, and if necessary cuffs and shackles, which feel about the same in the twenty-first century as they did in the nineteenth.

How Americans would view these things if the Big House had never existed, no one can tell. Yet it's a fact that in American popular culture, prisons are almost always seen in the light of Big House words and images.

The inescapable phrase, whenever prisons are mentioned—the phrase continually used by talk shows, blogs, and news reports—is "doing hard time." *Hard time* originated in the Big House period as a convict term for psychological suffering, for taking your incarceration to heart and really worrying about it. Now it is a universal synonym for "going to prison" or even "going to jail," as if every incarceration should be seen as a reenactment of the toughest features of the Big House regime. The words *Big House* are also in constant use, especially in documentaries about prison life, which can be seen at any hour of the day or night on cable television. Even when these shows have to do with institutions that were built only recently, they continually resort to Big House images and concepts. The camera lingers on barred doors, shackled limbs, convict uniforms, and other familiar expressions of Big House art. *Law and Order* (1990–), America's favorite crime show, specializes in small sets and noir lighting, but when it deals with convicts, it makes certain that Big

House symbolism gets the spotlight. Characters who are sentenced to prison are viewed as leaving for a separate world, the antithesis of normal life; and whenever they are summoned from that world, they look and sound as if they had come from a hermetically sealed Big House environment. They wear tall black numbers on their chests (stamped on huge white labels, for better visibility), and they frequently assert that no one on the Outside can possibly understand what life on the Inside is really like.

One of penology's recent innovations is the "private prison," an institution (usually small) that is managed by a corporation under contract to the state. In practice, these places differ little from other modern prisons. But in the popular computer game Prison Tycoon, they also differ little from the Big House—an artificial world, maintaining itself against the forces that naturally tend toward its destruction. Players of Prison Tycoon face the challenge of chapters 2 and 6—that of building a Big House, "Brick by Brick," and then running it. "Start from the ground up," they're advised, "placing the very walls and fences that will house and contain your prisoners. Choose from multiple isolated environments and get to work. Determine the overall security level of your lockdown, but beware! Too harsh a prison will create a dangerous environment and could spark prisoner riots. Too lenient an approach will result in rampant gang activity. . . . Influence prisoner morale by creating prison industries including . . . chain gangs and farming. Just remember, new jobs mean new opportunities for escape."[33] Any substantial, though artificially created, world requires people to make choices and to pay for them. In this sense, the Big House remains substantial, even in its virtual form.

Other games are more contemporary in language, but they also derive their interest from perennial Big House themes, or what are assumed to be such. Prison Bitch, a card game, invites players to adopt the identities of various convict characters—rated by standards of "Toughness," "Reputation," and "Money"—and then to "use wealth, popularity, strength and pure viciousness to dominate all other inmates and make them your 'Bitches.'" Characters have to confront Big House obstacles, which if not surmounted will result in the loss of "Reputation Points."[34] "Toughness" is what the Big House was always supposed to embody, and that is still its "Reputation." The Big House survives, in imagination, as a haven for qualities that people imagine they can acquire once they cross the boundary from normal society into a separate world where nobody doubts that toughness is a virtue.

Meanwhile, as in the nineteenth century, literal Big Houses continue to gratify their visitors. Old prisons have been turned into museums in California, Montana, Wyoming, Colorado, Ohio, West Virginia, Pennsylvania, and probably, by the time you read this book, in other states as well. In my experience, today's tourists always replicate the distinctive combination of responses that the Big House used to elicit from its civilian guests: "This is really amazing!" and "I'm just glad I don't have to live here myself!" Neither response is unfavorable to the Big House idea. And many relics of the Big House period are still in operation (Jackson, or parts of it, Stateville, San Quentin, Sing Sing, Elmira, and numerous others)—their "stupefying vastness" still remarkable, even to people who are used to remarkable sights.[35]

There have, of course, been modifications, changes that are bound to offend iconic sensibilities. In the 1980s the state of Illinois destroyed three of Stateville's great panopticons, charging that they "pose[d] unique management problems"—although the one circular cellhouse that still exists works very well, thank you, according to its officers and inmates. More sensibly, if not more artistically, the state divided the great circular mess hall into several sections.[36] Warden Ragen's glorious garden has been replaced by a wide expanse of dirt, with podular buildings growing out of it—ugliness unrelieved by any sense of theater.

But it's not true that "people-processing institution[s]"—prisons—have been "demystif[ied]," as a historian of Stateville once speculated.[37] The very notion of "processing" human beings is a gift from Big House rituals of initiation and transformation, rituals that continue in operation, though without the haughty self-assurance of the original Big House. And "demystification" is not the same as "criticism." What is the significance of saying that something has been "demystified," when it continues to inspire both fantasy and respect?

In any event, the idea and image of the Big House are impossible to destroy. In the TV series *Prison Break* (2005–9) everything has been done to evoke the charisma that men acquire from struggling inside a cagelike prison; it was that kind of charisma (not the ludicrous plot) that won the show its large audience. But to make such dramas work, there has to be a sufficiently impressive cage. To get one, the producers went back to the old, abandoned Joliet State Prison, six miles from renovated Stateville, to a place that retains the art of a nineteenth-century Big House: giant stone cellblocks and Victorian-gothic towers, and the forbidding air of isolation that signifies that something serious must be going on Inside. "*That*," as a corrections official told me about Joliet, "is a *real* prison."

No doubt about it. Nothing can rival the impression of a true Big House. And the impression is based on reality. Even today, when you are sentenced to a real prison, you will arrive wearing cuffs and shackles, and you will be numbered, uniformed, and locked inside a cage of some kind. You will become a convict; and the tougher the prison, the tougher and more significant your experience will be.

A recent book, written from the other side of the officer-inmate divide, presents a realistic examination of the problems involved in guarding the Big House, as it used to be and still is in many places in America. The author describes his service as an officer in one of the old wall towers at Sing Sing, where he was armed with tear gas, a shotgun, a revolver, and an assault rifle, in case any problems came up. Yet as he looked out of the tower and over the prison, he felt something that was more important to express than to demystify: "I loved the architecture. . . . I loved the breeze blowing through, and my privileged position firmly astride the prison wall, with both sides in plain view."[38] It's possible that only the Big House could show you both sides of life, so clearly, and with so little intention of compromise.

In 1999 Florida demolished its pint-sized Big House, built in 1928. Modern equipment was expected to make short work of it. But the first swings of the wrecking ball "didn't make a dent. . . . The ball just bounced off."[39] The building was just that tough.

Notes

Touring the Institution

1. Cather, *O Pioneers!* 280–84.
2. Johnston, *Forms of Constraint*, 74; Lewis, *Development of American Prisons*, 91, 188; Keve, *Prisons and the American Conscience*, 59–60; Lawes, *20,000 Years in Sing Sing*, 66–67, 114.
3. *Kansas State Industrial Reformatory*, 44; Moore, "Two Years of Achievement," 8; McGraw and McGraw, *Assignment: Prison Riots*, 222. Rector, *Health and Medical Service*, 224–25, comments on the public's frequent attendance at prison concerts.
4. Postcard of Clinton Prison (New York), postmarked July 8, 1904; author's collection.
5. Mason, "Relocating Hollywood's Prison Film Discourse," 195.
6. Lighter, *Random House Historical Dictionary*, 149. The phrase seems to have appeared in print for the first time in 1913.
7. Lawes, *Life and Death*, xiv; Cahalan, *Historical Corrections Statistics*, 29; Lerner, *Historical Statistics*, 1141–42. In 1880 and 1890, however, the army had been much less populous than the prisons.
8. Garrett and MacCormick, *Handbook of American Prisons*, 32, 19, 739, 157,

185

475, 533, 260, 269, 760, 788, 147, 310, 301, 279; Rector, *Health and Medical Service*, 244. Prisons can usually be identified, as in this passage, by their location, although sometimes more than one prison has succeeded another in the same community; and prisons have often been renamed, or called by various names, even by the people who run them. There are formal names and colloquial names. Thus Michigan's largest prison has been called Jackson Prison, Jackson prison, the Michigan State Prison, the State Prison of Southern Michigan, Jacktown, and so on. This book can't settle all the issues of nomenclature, but I will try to be clear about which institutions I am discussing.

9. Hale, *Police and Prison Cyclopaedia*, 69–157. The proportions for c. 1930 and c. 1890 grow even larger (to about one-half) when one excludes southern states that preferred prison farms or work gangs to penitentiaries.

10. Hale, *Police and Prison Cyclopaedia*, 69–157; *New York State Reformatory*, D1.

11. Cunningham, *Castle*, 16–18, 22–25.

12. Wetmore, "Life in a Great Prison," 58.

13. "What It's Like to Be Behind Bars at Sing Sing," *Foto-rama*, March 1953, 122–29; "Opening of New Georgia Prison Marks Beginning of the Chain Gang's End," *Life*, September 20, 1937, 35.

14. Martin, "America's Toughest Prison," 21; Manly and Wright, *World of Its Own*, 2–4. For Joliet's dimensions, see Garrett and MacCormick, *Handbook of American Prisons*, 259.

15. Matthews, "Southern Michigan Prison," 5; "Holstein-Friesian Herd at Prison Largest in World," *Jackson Citizen Patriot*, July 24, 1927; *Photo Tour of M.S.P.*, unnumbered page; Urdaburn, "Chino," 11. For another example of the "city" motif, see O'Neill and Steinheimer, "San Quentin," 116.

16. Prison population growth: Sabol, "Prison and Jail Inmates," 2; Cahalan, *Historical Corrections Statistics*, 30.

17. Manly and Wright, *World of Its Own*; Havemann, "Paradox," 85.

18. Quotation from O'Neill and Steinheimer, "San Quentin," 116.

19. Morris, *Devil's Butcher Shop*, 31–32.

20. Quotations from Lewis, "Attica Prison."

21. On the creation and propagation of icons, see Cox, "*Titanic*," and Cox, "Biblical Icon."

22. Gerber et al., *Hard Time*, no. 2 (2004), 6.

23. Barnes, *History*, 614, quoting a report (1890) by a reformatory commission to the governor of New Jersey; Brockway, *Fifty Years of Prison Service*, 163.

24. Carter et al., *Historical Statistics*, 5.256–57; Colvin, *Penitentiaries*, 167–68.

TWO

How to Build a Big House

1. Lawes, *20,000 Years in Sing Sing*, 85–86; Johnston, *Human Cage*, 40; Johnston, *Forms of Constraint*, 77. An authoritative description appears in "Presentment of the Westchester County Grand Jury [on] Conditions of Sing Sing Prison" (1913), in Tannenbaum, *Osborne of Sing Sing*, 323–36.

2. Tocqueville and Beaumont, *On the Penitentiary System*, 76; Lawes, *20,000 Years in Sing Sing*, 73.

3. Lewis, *Development of American Prisons*, 124.

4. Ibid., 240, 246–49. Lewis places a bizarre faith in the insanity statistics.

5. Tocqueville and Beaumont, *On the Penitentiary System*, 72–79, 164, 165; Brian, *Sing Sing*, 27, 44; Lawes, *20,000 Years in Sing Sing*, 88–89; "Prison Management," *Appleton's Journal*, October 16, 1869, 280.

6. Pisciotta, *Benevolent Repression*, 160.

7. Johnston, *Forms of Constraint*, 62–63; Lewis, *Development of American Prisons*, 237, 239; Tocqueville and Beaumont, *On the Penitentiary System*, 212.

8. Lewis, *Development of American Prisons*, 121, quoting a description of 1829; Tocqueville and Beaumont, *On the Penitentiary System*, 103–4.

9. Wines, *State of Prisons*, 171.

10. Klein, *Prison Methods*, 122–23.

11. Four of many examples: "Convicts Riot, Put Torch to Auburn Prison," *New York Times*, July 29, 1929; Garrett and MacCormick, *Handbook of American Prisons*, 844; Martin, *Break Down the Walls*, 187, 214; "Stone upon Stone," *Time*, November 18, 1929.

12. Banka, *State Prison Life*, 87, 19.

13. Hopkins, *Prisons and Prison Building*, 45, 138–39.

14. Keve, *Prisons and the American Conscience*, 38, 40–41, 53; Barnes, *History*, 287–89; Hopkins, *Prisons and Prison Building*, facing 49; "Big Dome at Rahway," *New York Times*, August 14, 1897. In fact, Rahway's dome was shorter, though larger in diameter, than the Capitol's.

15. Barnum, *Jail Cells*, 2.

16. Garrett and MacCormick, *Handbook of American Prisons*, 758; Manly and Wright, *World of Its Own*, 14; Jacobs, *Stateville*, 16.

17. Wetmore, "Life in a Great Prison," 58.

18. At least according to the vague statements of McKelvey, *American Prisons*, 157.

19. Garrett and MacCormick, *Handbook of American Prisons*, 709, 161; Lamott, *Chronicles of San Quentin*, 182; "Model Prison of the World Opened at Joliet," *Aurora* [Illinois] *Sunday Beacon-News*, December 7, 1924.

20. Ed Ward, letter to Warden Macgowan, Maine State Prison, August 15, 1937 (manuscript, author's collection), 5.

21. New York State Special Commission, *Attica*, 373; Useem and Kimball, *States of Siege*, 29–55.

22. Quotation from Morris, *Devil's Butcher Shop*, 34; riot account ibid. and from Useem and Kimball, *States of Siege*, 86–87, 101–3, 105–6.

23. Evans, *Fabrication of Virtue*, 218–20. Evans's book is the most lucid source I have found for Bentham's prison projects.

24. Foucault, *Discipline and Punish*, esp. 205–6.

25. Hopkins, *Prisons and Prison Building*, 43.

26. Penitentiary Commission, *New Illinois State Penitentiary*, 4; Illinois Department of Corrections, *Illinois State Penitentiary*, 5; Zimmerman, Saxe, and Zimmerman, *New Illinois State Penitentiary*, 10, 22–23.

27. Manly and Wright, *World of Its Own*, 13.

28. Martin, *Break Down the Walls*, 134–35.

29. Martin, "America's Toughest Prison," 56.

30. Garrett and MacCormick, *Handbook of American Prisons*, 836, 845; Special Committee, "Michigan Prison Riots," 7–8.

31. Bright, *Powers That Punish*, 62–63, 93; postcard, author's collection.

32. Alcatraz population: Keve, *Prisons and the American Conscience*, 302.

33. Fifteen hundred forty-six convicts were imprisoned on Alcatraz during its twenty-nine years as the Rock (Esslinger, *Alcatraz*, 417), with roughly three hundred in residence at any given time.

34. Ibid., 72, 146; Keve, *Prisons and the American Conscience*, 179.

THREE

Your Life as a Convict

1. Grady, *Behind 30 Foot Walls!* 15.

2. McKelvey, *American Prisons*, 155; Blumenthal, *Miracle at Sing Sing*, 149;

Leopold, *Life Plus 99 Years*, 84. Here, as elsewhere in this narrative of prison life, a composite picture is being created from many examples of general customs. Head shaving was common in jails and prisons throughout America until the mid-twentieth century, when it became generally unfashionable in the North. It is still common in southern prisons.

3. Chamberlin, "In a State Prison," 259.

4. Cover illustrations, *Frank Leslie's Illustrated Newspaper*, March 10, 1888; Wetmore, "New System."

5. Jackson, *Killing Time*, 15.

6. Neese, *Prison Exposures*, 44; Leopold, *Life Plus 99 Years*, 87.

7. Lawes, *20,000 Years in Sing Sing*, illustration facing 108.

8. Kantrowitz, *Close Control*, 60–61.

9. McKelvey, *American Prisons*, 155–56; Lawes, *Life and Death*, 70; Giles, *Jerry's Riot*, 4.

10. Touhy, *Stolen Years*, 226.

11. Chamberlin, "In a State Prison," 259.

12. Brian, *Sing Sing*, 61; McGraw and McGraw, *Assignment: Prison Riots*, 219; Fishman, *Sex in Prison*, 90.

13. Bauman and Ehrlich, "They Don't Escape," 23; Clemmer, *Prison Community*, 75.

14. Neese, *Prison Exposures*, 45.

15. Grand jury report, in Tannenbaum, *Osborne of Sing Sing*, 335.

16. Kantrowitz, *Close Control*, 68; Fishman, *Sex in Prison*, illustration facing 128.

17. Wilson, "S.M.P. Laundry" (1939). See also "Laundry Washes 20-Tons Of Clothes Weekly; Loses Few," *Spectator*, January 8, 1944; Ashley and Button, "Laundry Problems" (1989).

18. Lewis, *Development of American Prisons*, presents as much significant information as one can expect to find on this subject—but see also the claims of Brockway, *Fifty Years of Prison Service*, 31, 59.

19. "Prison Management," *Appleton's Journal*, October 16, 1869, 280–81.

20. Reimer, "Socialization in the Prison Community," 154; Sykes, *Society of Captives*, 31; Clemmer, *Prison Community*, 275.

21. Nelson, *Prison Days and Nights*, 12.

22. Litchfield, *Official Report*, 12; also Leopold, *Life Plus 99 Years*, 149–50, describing the double-door punishment at Joliet, which was still being administered in the 1920s.

23. In 1853, Auburn Penitentiary provided 223 "shower baths" and 88 "yok-

ings": Klein, *Prison Methods*, 212–14. See also Rosenberg, *Wonders of the World*, 495–97.

24. According to a survey with forty-four prisons reporting (Hale, *Police and Prison Cyclopaedia*, 163).

25. Clemmer, *Prison Community*, 204.

26. Lawes, *20,000 Years in Sing Sing*, 27.

27. Jim Blodgett, interview.

28. Leopold, *Life Plus 99 Years*, 87; Bennett, "Guest Editorial," 2.

29. Clemmer, *Prison Community*, 156–57, commenting on the quoted convict's observation.

30. Dudding, *Trail of the Dead Years*, illustration section after 118. The picture represents the West Virginia Penitentiary about 1910.

FOUR

The Art of Humiliation

1. Neese, *Prison Exposures*, 37.

2. Sykes, *Society of Captives*, 21.

3. Erickson, *Warden Ragen of Joliet*, 44; Goffman, *Asylums*, 111.

4. Quoted in McGraw and McGraw, *Assignment: Prison Riots*, 47. The recent popularity of the induction cut may result in part, however, from the transformation of Big House styles into symbols of ironically triumphant masculinity.

5. McCoy, "Prison Without Stripes."

6. There is, perhaps, only one official uniform that has maintained its place in American imagery more tenaciously than prison stripes. During the 1970s the U.S. Navy tried to replace its traditional sailor suits with modern shirts and trousers. It mounted a big publicity campaign, only to find that the more the new uniforms were advertised, the fewer enlistments occurred. The old masculine-feminine suits, with their flap collars, bell-bottom trousers, and strange little caps, turned out to be sexually potent. This story is told in part by Fussell, *Uniforms* (30–32), who adds some brief and not conspicuously accurate comments about prison uniforms (121–22).

7. Klein, *Prison Methods*, 152; Lewis, *Development of American Prisons*, 58, 90.

8. Wetmore, "Life in a Great Prison," 58; Chamberlin, "In a State Prison," 259; Klein, *Prison Methods*, 152–53; Hopp et al., *Michigan State Prison*, 17, 19.

9.   Lawes, *Life and Death*, 56, illustration facing 58.

10. Chamberlin, "In a State Prison," 259.

11. Tasker, *Grimhaven*, 9–10; Lawes, *20,000 Years in Sing Sing*, 100; Lawes, *Life and Death*, 56.

12. Leopold, *Life Plus 99 Years*, 84. The clothes-that-don't-fit scene is reen-acted in *Prison Mutiny* (1943), with much the same implications about what convicts can expect from prison.

13. Duffy, *San Quentin Story*, 67–68.

14. Ibid., 67.

15. Thus Clemmer, *Prison Community*, 102, on the prison at Chester, Illinois. Clemmer was a good scholar of prisons, but he exaggerates here, having fallen under the spell of the all-powerful prison number.

16. Jacobs, *Stateville*, 191.

17. Michigan Department of Corrections, *Annual Report* (1998), 20–22; (1999), 70–71; (2001), 1, 31.

18. "Men with Numbers": O'Neill and Steinheimer, "San Quentin," 118–19.

19. Elliott, "World Within Walls," 70.

20. Postcard, postmarked June 22, 1951, author's collection.

21. Parish, *Prison Pictures from Hollywood*, published a decade ago, lists 293 theatrical and television films, but prison has been an important element of many more productions.

22. Clemmer, *Prison Community*, 169.

FIVE

Sex

1.   Eigenberg and Baro, in "If You Drop the Soap in the Shower," examine "serious" films of the past few decades and speculate in a similar way about them.

2.   Mariner, *No Escape*, and O'Donnell, "Prison Rape in Context," present useful reviews of the literature and comment appropriately on problems involved in speculating about the incidence of rape and homosexual rela-tions—although their own analyses need to be viewed from the same critical distance as the data they consider. Some of Mariner's conclusions appear to be based on only about two hundred prisoner reports. See also Hensley, Koscheski, and Tewksbury, "Impact of Institutional Factors" (which illustrates the wild variety of statistics that it is possible to gener-

ate on this subject), and Eigenberg and Baro, "If You Drop the Soap in the Shower." Relevant to speculation about the frequency of homosexual relations in prison is an extraordinarily large study of inmates in the Georgia prison system, which revealed extraordinarily low rates of transmission of the AIDS virus. Kunzel, *Criminal Intimacy*, 304–6, and Brown, "Few Men Found to Get HIV in Prison," review the evidence.

3. Martin, *Break Down the Walls*, 177–79.

4. Jim Blodgett, interview; Neese, *Prison Exposures*, 52.

5. *Rules and Instructions* 11; Kantrowitz, *Close Control*, 152–53, and communication to author.

6. Yet nineteenth-century prisons often reported very small numbers of men sentenced for "sodomy" or the "crime against nature" (Hale, *Police and Prison Cyclopaedia*, 83, 85).

7. In 1970 officials at Jackson labored to suppress a large gang of convicts who were threatening others with rape, and sometimes acting on the threat. There were ethnic issues involved, as well as issues of power and money; but some (at least) of the aggressors were gay, in the usual sense of the term. Detailed historical data on these matters are rare; data on this case can be found in the Warden's Files, Archives of Michigan. Kunzel, *Criminal Intimacy*, offers a discussion of the literature on sexual assaults in prison but draws no general conclusions about the nature of these assaults, whether "erotic" or "aggressive" or both; and she is reluctant to call "same-sex sex" acts "homosexual." This does little to address the central issue of feeling and motive. It continues the old convict custom (which has become the new custom among some academic theorists) of disassociating sexual aggressors from conventionally "gay" erotic feelings.

8. Tannenbaum, *Osborne of Sing Sing*, 37, 330.

9. Pisciotta, *Benevolent Repression*, 101; Tannenbaum, *Osborne of Sing Sing*, 330, 335; Havemann, "Paradox of the Prisons," 98; Osborne, *Prisons and Common Sense*, 88–93.

10. Fishman, *Sex in Prison*, 151, 83.

11. Blumenthal, *Miracle at Sing Sing*, 48–49; Brian, *Sing Sing*, 75–78; Tannenbaum, *Osborne of Sing Sing*, 330.

12. Hanlon, *Classification and Treatment*, 11; Hanlon and Christian, *Resume of the Activities*, 6.

13. Martin, "America's Toughest Prison," 58; Manly and Wright, *World of Its Own*, 19; Duffy, *San Quentin Story*, 150–51. In 1916 segregated homosex-

uals in New York prisons also numbered 2 percent (Kunzel, *Criminal Intimacy*, 81–82).

14. Kinsey, *Sexual Behavior*, 529, 664, thought that between 30 and 85 percent of male inmates had at least one homosexual encounter, and the same was true for almost 40 percent of all males.

15. See also Kunzel, *Criminal Intimacy*, 103.

16. A rare prison book that is richly informed by the opinions of a local community regards homosexuality as a "common and sometimes, hardly clandestine" feature of a 1950s Big House (Giles, *Jerry's Riot*, 287).

17. Ed Ward, letter to Warden Macgowan, Maine State Prison, August 15, 1937 (manuscript, author's collection), 1, 4.

18. Clemmer, *Prison Community*, 89.

19. Lamott, *Chronicles of San Quentin*, 200.

20. Berkman, *Prison Memoirs*, 430–40, 450.

21. Nelson, *Prison Days and Nights*, 140–69.

22. Fishman, *Sex in Prison*, 5, 7.

23. Ibid., 150–53, 33.

24. Ibid., 85–89.

25. Clemmer, *Prison Community*, 249–73.

26. Wey, "Physician's Report," 100–101; Rector, *Health and Medical Service*, 178–79; Brockway, *Fifty Years of Prison Service*, 213–23; *Indiana Reformatory*, 3.

27. "Brockway on the Stand," *New York Sun*, September 13, 1894; "The Reformatory a Model," *New York Sun*, December 11, 1894; *New York State Reformatory*, D1; Brockway, *Fifty Years of Prison Service*, 14.

28. The "January deal," the Osborne accusation, and the publicity that came out of them long predate a scandal at New York's Welfare Island prison that is said to have "brought sex in prison into broad public view for the first time" (Kunzel, *Criminal Intimacy*, 77).

29. McGraw and McGraw, *Assignment: Prison Riots*, 91. The major unresearched subject is homosexual relations between inmates and staff. Prison wardens minimize its frequency, as does Fishman, *Sex in Prison*, 72–75. Perhaps they are right, although contrary evidence occasionally surfaces; see, for instance, Bright, *Powers That Punish*, 83, and Scudder, *Prisoners Are People*, 180–86. A writer who investigated Sing Sing by working as a guard suggests that homosexual rape is less common in prison than consensual sex between inmates and today's female guards (Conover, *Newjack*, 263).

30. My account of the riot at Jackson is drawn largely from McGraw and Mc-Graw, *Assignment: Prison Riots*, 91, 97; Martin, *Break Down the Walls*, 80–83; and Fox, *Violence Behind Bars*, 89, 93, 137, 242–43, 252. Bright, *Powers That Punish*, 208–9, summarizes substantial but conflicting testimony. The film is *Jacktown* (1962). In kindred events during the riot at the Montana State Prison in 1959, inmates raped other inmates and forced captive officers to watch (Giles, *Jerry's Riot*, 316).

31. "Correspondent Drags Out Skeleton," *Spectator*, November 28, 1938. Debate continues in the December 5 and 12 issues.

32. Moore, "Two Years of Achievement," 6, illustration caption, 12; Special Committee, "Michigan Prison Riots," 35.

33. Sykes, *Society of Captives*, 71.

34. Kunzel, *Criminal Intimacy*, 140, notes that movies about women's prisons ordinarily use the "iconography of men's prison movies."

35. Contrast *Oz*, with its preposterous extremes of violence, with *On the Yard* (1979), a prison movie in which even the con boss, a loan shark and drug dealer who in the course of business has other prisoners viciously attacked, reacts to a proposal to kill a young "punk," the junior member of a gay couple, by saying, "Be cool. He's not hurtin' us." Times have changed. Even real prison violence can't compete with today's attempts to represent it "realistically" on film. Even the violent "realism" of some comic book treatments of prison (see Gerber et al., *Hard Time*) is less megaviolent than *Oz*.

36. A broad statement, capable of only broad application. Among the institutional exceptions are, of course, the military and, to some extent, hospitals, secret intelligence agencies, and the presidency. But although many people fetishize power and money, few fetishize the Ford Motor Company or the Commerce Department.

SIX

You Built It, Now Try to Run It

1. Rhodes, *Total Confinement*, is an excellent example of a Foucauldian work that offers non-Foucauldian evidence. Pisciotta, *Benevolent Repression*, 61, 79, appears to share my view of Foucault, Brockway, et alia.

2. Martin, *Break Down the Walls*, 175.

3. When Alcatraz was in its planning stages, three young female athletes demonstrated that they could easily swim to the island, but the untrained

convicts who attempted the reverse trip never made good their escapes—myth and speculation to the contrary (Keve, *Prisons and the American Conscience*, 176, 183–84).

4. Beacher, *Alcatraz Island*, 77–91.

5. Martin, *Break Down the Walls*, 214; "Stabs Warden at Prayer," *New York Times*, February 12, 1912; "Convicts Mutiny," *New York Times*, March 15, 1912.

6. Sykes, *Society of Captives*, 46.

7. At the start of the Great Depression, prison officers in Michigan were doing relatively well: they received about thirty thousand dollars a year, in today's money, for their risky occupation. By 1938, however, their pay had fallen to about twenty-one thousand. They could take only two days off a month. No pension system was in place (Wood, *One Hundred Years*, 205, 231–32).

8. Keve, *Prisons and the American Conscience*, 68–70.

9. Irwin, *Prisons in Turmoil*, 15.

10. Tocqueville and Beaumont, *On the Penitentiary System* (60, 200), observing Sing Sing in the early 1830s, thought that if convicts were even allowed to speak, "the life of the keepers would be at the[ir] mercy."

11. Lawes, *20,000 Years in Sing Sing*, 96.

12. Beacher, *Alcatraz Island*, 176–83.

13. "Killer's Prison Video Sparks Illinois Lawmakers Outrage," *New York Times*, May 16, 1996; anonymous source, interview.

14. Kunzel, *Criminal Intimacy*, 160.

15. Edgerton, *Montana Justice*, 84, 144n50.

16. Brockway, *Fifty Years of Prison Service*, 178, 34–40; Erickson, *Warden Ragen of Joliet*, 96.

17. Lawes, *Life and Death*, 76–77; Garrett and MacCormick, *Handbook of American Prisons*, 706.

18. Scudder, *Prisoners Are People*, 195, Wilson and Barnes, "Riot," 150; Giles, *Jerry's Riot*, 178, 180; Useem and Kimball, *States of Siege*, 166; Banka, *State Prison Life*, 265, 270.

19. Purves, *Nightkeeper's Reports*, 51, 59–60, 62, 63–64, 77; Clark, *Lockstep and Corridor*, 50.

20. Wood, *One Hundred Years*, 95–105, 238–44, 288–91.

21. Lamott, *Chronicles of San Quentin*, 222–26; Duffy, *San Quentin Story*, 47–53.

22. "3 Slain at Folsom Prison in Savage Fight to Escape," *New York Times*, September 20, 1937; "Folsom Warden Dies of Wounds," *New York Times*,

September 25, 1937; "Prison Riot Ends as Leader Kills Comrades, Then Self," *New York Times*, October 5, 1929.

23. Daniell, "Hold Warden Hostage," 1; "Warden Relates Story of Capture," *New York Times*, December 12, 1929; "Roosevelt to Act Jan. 1," *New York Times*, December 12, 1929.

24. Keve, *Prisons and the American Conscience*, 191–92.

25. Fox, *Violence Behind Bars*, 4–21.

26. Lamott, *Chronicles of San Quentin*, 250. Segregation was abolished in the mess hall only in 1960 (Cummins, *Rise and Fall*, 71).

27. Tasker, *Grimhaven*, 125–28; Lamott, *Chronicles of San Quentin*, 197–200, 143.

28. Sykes, *Society of Captives*, 122–29. For an example of the process, see Giles, *Jerry's Riot*, esp. 145–56.

29. Useem and Kimball, *States of Siege*, 218–22.

30. Rhodes, *Total Confinement*, 169.

31. Jim Blodgett, interview.

32. Lewis, *Development of American Prisons*, 202, 242.

33. Cahalan, *Historical Corrections Statistics*, 49–53; Wilson and Barnes, "Riot," 139.

34. Sykes, *Society of Captives*, xvii–xviii.

35. Cummins, *Rise and Fall*, 12–20.

36. Purves, *Nightkeeper's Reports*, 54; Litchfield, *Official Report*, 16, 34; "The Reformatory a Model," *New York Sun*, December 11, 1894.

37. "Wanted—A Heartless Man," *Erie* [Pennsylvania] *Evening Herald*, August 29, 1907.

38. Clemmer, *Prison Community*, 182–83, 205.

39. Martin, *Break Down the Walls*, 174.

40. Keegan, *Mask of Command*, 128; Tocqueville and Beaumont, *On the Penitentiary System*, 165, 216.

41. For one example of what virtually all the experts said, see "Prison Experts Urge 1,500 as Housing Limit," *New York Times*, September 13, 1929.

SEVEN

A Tale of Two Prisons

1. The (changing) rankings for "biggest prison" are a matter of population, physical size, and local publicity. In 1934 San Quentin boasted the highest population, 6,397; Jackson followed at 5,215; Stateville, whose num-

bers had been increasing, held 3,867. Warden Ragen claimed that in 1939 Stateville and the old prison at Joliet (population about 1,500 in 1900), which was administered jointly with it, were "the world's largest . . . in inmate population." In 1951 San Quentin's population was 4,742, Jackson's 6,272, of which about 5,000 were prisoners living inside the walls, the rest in outside work quarters. Stateville in the 1950s had about 3,200 men inside its walls, with another 1,200 at Joliet, yet it was still six acres larger than Jackson, just as Jackson was almost three times the physical size of San Quentin. See Bright, *Powers That Punish*, 43; Erickson, *Warden Ragen of Joliet*, 21; Garrett and MacCormick, *Handbook of American Prisons*, 155; Illinois Prison Inquiry Commission, *Prison System*, 158, 161; Jacobs, *Stateville*, 26; Lamott, *Chronicles of San Quentin*, 202; Ragen and Finston, *Inside the World's Toughest Prison*, v–vi; Special Committee, "Michigan Prison Riots," 7–8.

2. Erickson, *Warden Ragen of Joliet*, 42–48; Jacobs, *Statevillle*, 24–25; Leopold, *Life Plus 99 Years*, 146–47. The practice of canary keeping was very common in the Big House. For the warden of Sing Sing, it was part of his prison's "soul" (Lawes, *20,000 Years in Sing Sing*, illustration facing 109).

3. Sykes, *Society of Captives*, 127; Jacobs, *Statevillle*, 25.

4. Kantrowitz, *Close Control*, 193, 89–91; Pate, "Disciplinary Reports." Kantrowitz's book is a detailed study of the ways in which Ragen wielded power.

5. Bauman and Ehrlich, "They Don't Escape," 22.

6. Kantrowitz, *Close Control*, 193.

7. Ragen scrapbook, 1949 press reports; King, memo.

8. Kantrowitz, *Close Control*, 47–48, 66–67, 193. Kantrowitz, a modern liberal who might be expected to detest Ragen's regime, provides a powerful defense of it—and an indispensable study of the way in which a Big House actually operated.

9. Touhy, *Stolen Years*, 227.

10. Kantrowitz, *Close Control*, 40; Martin, "America's Toughest Prison."

11. Here, and elsewhere in this book, my basic sources on Jackson's history are Bright, *Powers That Punish*; Fox, *Violence Behind Bars*; and Rubenstein and Ziewacz, *Three Bullets Sealed His Lips*.

12. Martin, *Break Down the Walls*, 26, 32–34.

13. Ibid., 26–28, 32–34, 39.

14. Ibid., 21.

15. McIntyre, "Inmate Politicians"; "Convict, Guest at Party, Escapes from Jackson," *Detroit Free Press*, January 5, 1935.
16. Muller, "Bare Convict's Czarist Power"; Ewert, scrapbook.
17. "Lawes Inspects Prison: Sees It as One of Best in Country," *Spectator*, June 19, 1943.
18. Rubenstein and Ziewacz, *Three Bullets Sealed His Lips*; Rudow, "Parties, Gambling, Rackets."
19. Jackson State Prison Investigation, testimony, August 29, 1947; Bright, *Powers That Punish*, 242–43.
20. Wilson and Barnes, "Riot," 144.
21. Martin, *Break Down the Walls*, 87–88; Fox, *Violence Behind Bars*, 264–66.
22. Board of Inquiry, testimony of Earnest C. Brooks, May 2, 1952; Jackson State Prison Investigation, testimony of Harry Lanway.
23. Special Committee, "Michigan Prison Riots," 7–8.
24. Brockway, *Fifty Years of Prison Service*, 193–94.

E I G H T

Rajahs and Reformers

1. Brockway, *Fifty Years of Prison Service*, 14, 22, 85.
2. Ibid., 64–65; Barnes, *History*, 606; Lawes, *20,000 Years in Sing Sing*, 37.
3. Brockway, *Fifty Years of Prison Service*, 288–92; *New York State Reformatory*, H5.
4. Litchfield, *Official Report*, 34.
5. Nelson, *Prison Days and Nights*, 141.
6. Osborne, *Within Prison Walls*, 161, 183; Chamberlain, *There Is No Truce*, 241–47.
7. Tannenbaum, *Osborne of Sing Sing*, 265, 268, 234; Murphy, *Political Manhood*, 125–70.
8. Lawes, *20,000 Years in Sing Sing*, 66–67.
9. Dolan and Bogdanovich, "Candid Camera Dupes Critics." The series won a prestigious journalism award (Columbia University news release, January 20, 1999).
10. Bagdikian, *Shame of the Prisons*; Reimer, "Socialization in the Prison Community."
11. Murton, *Accomplices to the Crime*, xiv.
12. Ibid., 136.
13. Sources for Fox's story are his own book, *Violence Behind Bars*, checked

198

against Bright, *Powers That Punish*; Martin, *Break Down the Walls*; and Mc-Graw and McGraw, *Assignment: Prison Riots*.

14. Chamberlain, *There Is No Truce*, 295.

15. Fox, *Violence Behind Bars*, 142–43.

16. Elli, *Riot*, 151.

17. *Time*, November 18, 1929; Blumenthal, *Miracle at Sing Sing*, 245–46. On at least one occasion, Lawes eased his literary labors by simply copying the work of another author; see Lawes, *Life and Death*, chapter 9, with its misleading acknowledgment (222) of Lewis, *Development of American Prisons*, chapters 10 and 12.

18. Erickson, *Warden Ragen of Joliet*.

19. Ragen and Finston, *Inside the World's Toughest Prison*.

20. Ragen, "Life and 99 Years." Ragen also attempted a general history of punishment, "The Devil Stoned," which never passed the manuscript stage.

21. Tannenbaum, *Osborne of Sing Sing*, 143.

22. Blumenthal, *Miracle at Sing Sing*, 152; Duffy, *San Quentin Story*, 146–47; O'Neill and Steinheimer, "San Quentin," 119.

23. *Duffy of San Quentin*, 5.

24. Manly and Wright, *World of Its Own*, 2–4.

25. Ragen, "Life and 99 Years," 415–16, 340, 83–84; Brockway, *Fifty Years of Prison Service*, 126–35.

26. Blumenthal, *Miracle at Sing Sing*, 112–13, 155.

27. Lawes, *Sing Sing*, 1–6; Lawes, *20,000 Years in Sing Sing*, 307–8.

28. Blumenthal, *Miracle at Sing Sing*, 173.

29. Ibid., 98.

30. Cummins, *Rise and Fall*, esp. 11–20, 253.

NINE

Prisons You Can't Tear Down

1. Kunzel, *Criminal Intimacy*, 36–37.

2. My account of the events of Stroud's life relies on Babyak's well-researched biography, *Bird Man*.

3. Irwin, *Prisons in Turmoil*, 6.

4. Babyak, *Bird Man*, 192.

5. Bauman and Ehrlich, "They Don't Escape," 24, 20.

6. McGraw and McGraw, *Assignment: Prison Riots*, 5.

7.   Martin, *Break Down the Walls*, 268, 272–73.

8.   Cummins, *Rise and Fall*, ix, 124.

9.   McGraw and McGraw, *Assignment: Prison Riots*, 225–26.

10. See Cummins, *Rise and Fall*, 20, on the situation in California.

11. Martin, *Break Down the Walls*, 185–86.

12. Jacobs, *Stateville*, 82.

13. Cummins, *Rise and Fall*, ix–x; Manly and Wright, *World of Its Own*, 2.

14. Cummins, *Rise and Fall*, 209.

15. "Rifle Fire Repels Rush of Convicts in Ohio Outbreak," *New York Times*, April 30, 1930; "Convicts Riot, Put Torch to Auburn Prison," *New York Times*, July 29, 1929; "Governor Lays Prison Riots to Rigor of Baumes Laws; Acts to Stop Outbreaks," *New York Times*, July 30, 1929; Daniell, "Hold Warden Hostage," 1.

16. Cummins, *Rise and Fall*, 135, 240–42, et passim.

17. Kern, "Is This Any Way," 88.

18. Conte, *Is Prison Reform Possible?* esp. 26, 31–33, 69, 71.

19. McCoy, "Prison Without Stripes," 78. For the longer account of Washington, see McCoy and Hoffman, *Concrete Mama*.

20. McCoy, "Prison Without Stripes," 78.

21. Jacobs, *Stateville*, 166. The same thing happened in the riot at New Mexico in 1980 (Morris, *Devil's Butcher Shop*, 80, 121–22, 127, 137).

22. Jacobs, *Stateville*, esp. 73–104, 138–74; "Stateville Correctional Center —Now and Then," *Illinois Department of Corrections Perspectives* 4 (July–August 1983), 3.

23. Cressey, Foreword, vi–viii.

24. "Security of Custody," 1.

25. Useem and Kimball, *States of Siege*, 114–41.

26. Kalinich, *Inmate Economy*, 71. Kalinich's on-site research was conducted in 1976 and 1977.

27. "Daring Helicopter Raid Frees Convict," *Jackson Citizen Patriot*, June 7, 1975; Flory, "Budd Funeral." For killings in 1939 and 1960, see Matthews, "Reform at Pen," 7; Michigan Department of Corrections, "Fallen Employees."

28. Useem and Kimball, *States of Siege*, present the facts without reaching quite the same conclusions.

29. Johnson, "More Prisons Using Iron Hand."

30. Carter et al., *Historical Statistics*, 5.213–15, 5.256–57.

31. Cummins, *Rise and Fall*; Andersen, "What Are Prisons For?" Cressey,

Foreword, x, makes a roughly similar observation about the converging effects of liberal and conservative attitudes.

32. Oddly, Rhodes (*Total Confinement*, 14) finds supermax units "almost identical" to Bentham's panopticon.

33. ValuSoft, advertising material.

34. G-SpotGames.com, Prison Bitch rules and materials.

35. Conover, *Newjack*, 8, referring to Sing Sing's A-block, 588 feet long.

36. "Stateville Correctional Center," 3.

37. Jacobs, *Stateville*, 104, 118.

38. Conover, *Newjack*, 157–58.

39. [Florida Department of Corrections], "The Rock Tumbles Down," *Correctional Compass* 4 (April 1999), 1.

Works Cited

Abbreviations

ALL: Abraham Lincoln Presidential Library, Springfield, Illinois
AM: Archives of Michigan, Lansing
BHL: Bentley Historical Library, University of Michigan, Ann Arbor

Andersen, Kurt. "What Are Prisons For?" *Time*, September 13, 1982, 38–41.
Ashley, Carl, and Al Button. "Laundry Problems at SPSM." *Spectator*, August 1989, 1, 8.
Babyak, Jolene. *Bird Man: The Many Faces of Robert Stroud*. Berkeley: Ariel Vamp, 1994.
Bagdikian, Ben H. *The Shame of the Prisons*. New York: Pocket Books, 1972.
Banka, J. H. *State Prison Life, by One Who Has Been There*. Cincinnati: C. F. Vent, 1872.
Barnes, Harry Elmer. *A History of the Penal, Reformatory, and Correctional Institutions of the State of New Jersey: Analytical and Documentary*. Trenton: MacCrellish and Quigley, 1918.
E. T. Barnum Iron Works. *Jail Cells* [advertising circular]. Detroit: E. T. Barnum, [c. 1895].

Works Cited

Bauman, Frank, and Henry Ehrlich. "They Don't Escape from Joliet." *Look*, January 6, 1948, 20–27.

Beacher, Milton Daniel. *Alcatraz Island: Memoirs of a Rock Doc.* Newcastle upon Tyne: Zymurgy, 2003.

Bennett, L. "Guest Editorial" from the *Virginian. Spectator,* January 1, 1944, 2.

Berkman, Alexander. *Prison Memoirs of an Anarchist.* New York: Mother Earth, 1912.

Blumenthal, Ralph. *Miracle at Sing Sing.* New York: St. Martin's, 2004.

Board of Inquiry, Southern Michigan Prison Riot, 1952. Transcripts of Testimony, 1952. G. Mennen Williams Papers, box 106, BHL.

Brian, Denis. *Sing Sing: The Inside Story of a Notorious Prison.* Amherst NY: Prometheus, 2005.

Bright, Charles. *The Powers That Punish: Prison and Politics in the Era of the "Big House," 1920–1955.* Ann Arbor: University of Michigan Press, 1996.

Brockway, Zebulon Reed. *Fifty Years of Prison Service: An Autobiography.* 1912; rpt. Montclair NJ: Patterson Smith, 1969.

Brown, David. "Few Men Found to Get HIV in Prison." *Washington Post*, April 21, 2006.

Cahalan, Margaret Werner. *Historical Corrections Statistics in the United States, 1850–1984.* Rockville MD: Westat, 1986.

Carter, Susan B., et al. *Historical Statistics of the United States: Earliest Times to the Present.* New York: Cambridge University Press, 2006.

Cather, Willa. *O Pioneers!* In *Early Novels and Stories.* New York: Library of America, 1987.

Chamberlain, Rudolph W. *There Is No Truce: A Life of Thomas Mott Osborne.* New York: Macmillan, 1935.

Chamberlin, J. E. "In a State Prison." *Youth's Companion* 64 (April 30, 1891), 259.

Clark, Charles L. *Lockstep and Corridor: Thirty-five Years of Prison Life.* Cincinnati: University of Cincinnati Press, 1927.

Clemmer, Donald. *The Prison Community.* 1940. New York: Holt, Rinehart and Winston, 1958.

Colvin, Mark. *Penitentiaries, Reformatories, and Chain Gangs: Social Theory and the History of Punishment in Nineteenth-Century America.* New York: St. Martin's, 1997.

Conover, Ted. *Newjack: Guarding Sing Sing.* New York: Random House, 2000.

Conte, William R. *Is Prison Reform Possible?* Tacoma: Unique, 1990.

Cox, Stephen. "The Biblical Icon." In *Sacred History, Sacred Literature*, ed. Shawna Dolansky. Winona Lake IN: Eisenbrauns, 2008. Pp. 293–313.

———. "The *Titanic* and the Art of Myth." *Critical Review* 15 (Summer–Fall 2003), 403–34.

Cressey, Donald R. Foreword to Irwin, *Prisons in Turmoil*, vii–xi.

Cummins, Eric. *The Rise and Fall of California's Radical Prison Movement*. Stanford: Stanford University Press, 1994.

Cunningham, Bill. *Castle: The Story of a Kentucky Prison*. Kuttawa KY: McClanahan, 1995.

Daniell, Raymond. "Hold Warden Hostage." *New York Times*, December 12, 1929.

Dolan, Deirdre, and Peter Bogdanovich. "Candid Camera Dupes Critics." *New York Observer*, March 30, 1998.

Dudding, Earl Ellicott. *The Trail of the Dead Years*. Huntington WV: Prisoners Relief Society, 1932.

Duffy, Clinton T., as told to Dean Jennings. *The San Quentin Story*. Garden City NY: Doubleday, 1950.

Duffy of San Quentin. Warner Brothers advertising kit. Hollywood: Warner Brothers, 1954.

Edgerton, Keith. *Montana Justice: Power, Punishment, and the Penitentiary*. Seattle: University of Washington Press, 2004.

Eigenberg, Helen, and Agnes Baro. "If You Drop the Soap in the Shower You Are on Your Own: Images of Male Rape in Selected Prison Movies." *Sexuality and Culture* 7 (December 2003), 54–89.

Elli, Frank. *The Riot*. New York: Coward-McCann, 1966.

Elliott, Lawrence. "World Within Walls." *Coronet*, February 1952, 69–84.

Erickson, Gladys A. *Warden Ragen of Joliet*. New York: Dutton, 1957.

Esslinger, Michael. *Alcatraz: A Definitive History of the Penitentiary Years*. 3rd ed. San Francisco: OceanView, 2006.

Evans, Robin. *The Fabrication of Virtue: English Prison Architecture, 1750–1840*. Cambridge: Cambridge University Press, 1982.

Ewert, Albert Merritt. Scrapbook. Ewert Papers, AM.

Fishman, Joseph F. *Sex in Prison: Revealing Sex Conditions in American Prisons*. New York: National Library Press, 1934.

Flory, Bradley. "Budd Funeral." *Jackson Citizen Patriot*, December 31, 1987.

Foucault, Michel. *Discipline and Punish: The Birth of the Prison*. Trans. Alan Sheridan. 2nd ed. 1977; New York: Vintage, 1995.

Fox, Vernon. *Violence Behind Bars: An Explosive Report on Prison Riots in the United States.* New York: Vantage, 1956.

Fussell, Paul. *Uniforms: Why We Are What We Wear.* Boston: Houghton Mifflin, 2002.

Gaddis, Thomas E. *Birdman of Alcatraz: The Story of Robert Stroud.* New York: Random House, 1955.

Garrett, Paul W., and Austin H. MacCormick, eds. *Handbook of American Prisons and Reformatories, 1929.* New York: National Society of Penal Information, 1929.

Gerber, Steve, et al. *Hard Time.* New York: DC Comics, 2004–6.

Giles, Kevin S. *Jerry's Riot: The True Story of Montana's 1959 Prison Disturbance.* N.p.: Booklocker.com, 2005.

Goffman, Erving. *Asylums: Essays on the Social Situation of Mental Patients and Other Inmates.* Garden City NY: Anchor-Doubleday, 1961.

Grady, Leo. *Behind 30 Foot Walls!* Scrapbook. C. 1951. Author's collection.

G-SpotGames.com. Prison Bitch: The Card Game. 2003. Author's collection.

Hale, George W. *Police and Prison Cyclopaedia.* Rev. ed. Boston: Richardson, 1893.

Hanlon, Thomas J. *Classification and Treatment of the Youthful Delinquent at the Elmira Reformatory.* N.p.: n.p., [c. 1935].

Hanlon, Thomas J., and Frank L. Christian. *A Resume of the Activities Designed to Rehabilitate Youthful Delinquents Committed to the Elmira Reformatory.* N.p.: n.p., [c. 1937].

Havemann, Ernest. "The Paradox of the Prisons." *Life,* September 30, 1957, 84–86, 94, 96, 98, 100, 112, 115.

Hensley, Christopher, Mary Koscheski, and Richard Tewksbury. "The Impact of Institutional Factors on Officially Reported Sexual Assaults in Prisons." *Sexuality and Culture* 7 (December 2003), 16–26.

Hopkins, Alfred. *Prisons and Prison Building.* New York: Architectural Book Publishing, 1930.

Hopp, William F., et al. *The Michigan State Prison, Jackson, 1837–1928.* Jackson: Michigan State Prison, 1928.

Illinois Department of Corrections. *Illinois State Penitentiary: Joliet-Stateville Branch.* Springfield: State of Illinois, 1958.

Illinois Prison Inquiry Commission. *The Prison System in Illinois.* Springfield: State of Illinois, 1937.

Indiana Reformatory. Jeffersonville: Indiana Reformatory, [c. 1909].

Irwin, John. *Prisons in Turmoil.* Boston: Little, Brown, 1980.

Jackson, Bruce. *Killing Time: Life in the Arkansas Penitentiary*. Ithaca: Cornell University Press, 1977.

Jackson State Prison Investigation, 1947. Transcripts of testimony. Donald S. Leonard Collection, box 19, BHL.

Jacobs, James B. *Stateville: The Penitentiary in Mass Society*. Chicago: University of Chicago Press, 1977.

Johnson, Dirk. "More Prisons Using Iron Hand to Control Inmates." *New York Times*, November 1, 1990.

Johnston, Norman. *Forms of Constraint: A History of Prison Architecture*. Urbana: University of Illinois Press, 2000.

———. *The Human Cage: A Brief History of Prison Architecture*. New York: Walker, 1973.

Kalinich, David B. *The Inmate Economy*. Lexington MA: D. C. Heath, 1980.

Kansas State Industrial Reformatory. Hutchinson: Kansas State Industrial Reformatory, 1925.

Kantrowitz, Nathan. *Close Control: Managing a Maximum Security Prison, The Story of Ragen's Stateville Penitentiary*. Guilderland NY: Harrow and Heston, 1996.

Keegan, John. *The Mask of Command*. New York: Viking, 1987.

Kern, Edward. "Is This Any Way to Run a Prison?" *Life*, August 1979, 88.

Keve, Paul W. *Prisons and the American Conscience: A History of U.S. Federal Corrections*. Carbondale: Southern Illinois University Press, 1991.

King, Lt. C. Memo to Joseph E. Ragen, January 26, 1949. Ragen Papers, box 1, ALL.

Kinsey, Alfred C., et al. *Sexual Behavior in the Human Male*. Philadelphia: W. B. Saunders, 1948.

Klein Philip. *Prison Methods in New York State*. New York: Columbia University, 1920.

Kunzel, Regina. *Criminal Intimacy: Prison and the Uneven History of Modern American Sexuality*. Chicago: University of Chicago Press, 2008.

Lamott, Kenneth. *Chronicles of San Quentin: The Biography of a Prison*. New York: David McKay, 1961.

Lawes, Lewis E. *Life and Death in Sing Sing*. Garden City NY: Doubleday, 1928.

———. *Sing Sing*. N.p.: Strawberry-Hill, 1933.

———. *20,000 Years in Sing Sing*. New York: Ray Long and Richard R. Smith, 1932.

Leopold, Nathan F., Jr. *Life Plus 99 Years*. Garden City NY: Doubleday, 1958.

Lerner, William, ed. *Historical Statistics of the United States: From Colonial Times to 1970*. Washington: U.S. Government, 1975.

Lewis, Orlando F. *The Development of American Prisons and Prison Customs, 1776–1845*. New York: Prison Association of New York, 1922.

Lewis, Wilbur G. "Attica Prison to Be Convicts' Paradise." *New York Times*, August 2, 1931.

Lighter, J. E., ed. *Random House Historical Dictionary of American Slang*, vol. 1. New York: Random House, 1994.

Litchfield, Edward H. *The Official Report and Recommendations on the Investigation of the Elmira State Reformatory . . .* New York: New York World, 1894.

Manly, Chesly, and George Wright. *A World of Its Own: Inside Stateville Joliet Prisons*. Chicago: Chicago Tribune for the John Howard Association, [1955].

Mariner, Joanne. *No Escape: Male Rape in U.S. Prisons*. New York: Human Rights Watch, 2001.

Martin, John Bartlow. "America's Toughest Prison." *Saturday Evening Post*, October 20, 1951, 19–21, 52, 56, 58.

———. *Break Down the Walls: American Prisons: Present, Past, and Future*. New York: Ballantine, 1954.

Mason, Paul. "Relocating Hollywood's Prison Film Discourse." In *Captured by the Media: Prison Discourse in Popular Culture*, ed. Paul Mason. Cullompton, Devon: Willan, 2006. Pp. 191–209.

Matthews, Leland T. "Reform at Pen Still Question." *Jackson Citizen Patriot*, April 28, 1940.

———. "Southern Michigan Prison Operates Like a Large City." *Jackson Citizen Patriot*, April 22, 1940.

McCoy, John. "Prison Without Stripes." *Life*, August 1979, 78–87.

McCoy, John, and Ethan Hoffman. *Concrete Mama*. Columbia: University of Missouri Press, 1981.

McGraw, Peg, and Walter McGraw. *Assignment: Prison Riots*. New York: Henry Holt, 1954.

McIntyre, Thomas. "Inmate Politicians Rule Behind Jackson Walls." *Detroit News*, December 11, 1934.

McKelvey, Blake. *American Prisons: A Study in American Social History prior to 1915*. Chicago: University of Chicago Press, 1936.

Michigan Department of Corrections. *Annual Report*. Lansing: DOC, 1998, 1999, 2001.

———. "Fallen Employees." www.michigan.gov/corrections.

Moore, Joel R. "Two Years of Achievement." *Spectator,* January 15, 1939, supplement 1–12.

Morris, Roger. *The Devil's Butcher Shop: The New Mexico Prison Uprising.* Albuquerque: University of New Mexico Press, 1983.

Muller, Carl. "Bare Convict's Czarist Power at Jackson Prison." *Detroit Times,* July 21, 1933.

Murphy, Kevin P. *Political Manhood: Red Bloods, Mollycoddles, and the Politics of Progressive Era Reform.* New York: Columbia University Press, 2008.

Murton, Tom, with Joe Hyams. *Accomplices to the Crime.* New York: Grove, 1969.

Neese, Robert. *Prison Exposures.* Philadelphia: Chilton, 1959.

Nelson, Victor F. *Prison Days and Nights.* 1933. Garden City NY: Garden City Publishing, 1936.

New York State Reformatory at Elmira, Seventeenth Year Book. Elmira: N.Y.S. Reformatory Press, 1892.

New York State Special Commission on Attica. *Attica: The Official Report.* New York: Bantam, 1972.

O'Donnell, Ian. "Prison Rape in Context." *British Journal of Criminology* 44 (2004), 241–55.

O'Neill, Martin, and Charles E. Steinheimer. "San Quentin." *Life,* October 27, 1947, 116–25.

Osborne, Thomas Mott. *Prisons and Common Sense.* Philadelphia: Lippincott, 1924.

———. *Within Prison Walls.* New York: Appleton, 1914.

Parish, James Robert. *Prison Pictures from Hollywood.* Jefferson NC: McFarland, 2000.

Pate, Frank J. "Office of the Assistant Warden, Stateville Branch: Continuation of Disciplinary Reports." Memorandum. March 14, 1960. Ragen Papers, box 1, ALL.

Penitentiary Commission [Illinois]. *New Illinois State Penitentiary.* Joliet: Penitentiary Commission, 1924.

Photo Tour of M.S.P. [Michigan State Prison]. Jackson: State Prison of Southern Michigan, 1954.

Pisciotta, Alexander W. *Benevolent Repression: Social Control and the American Reformatory-Prison Movement.* New York: New York University Press, 1994.

Purves, John H. *The Nightkeeper's Reports, 1882.* Jackson MI: SPSM Spectator, 1954.

Ragen, Joseph E. *The Devil Stoned.* Unpublished typescript. Ragen Papers, box 4, ALL.

———. "Life and 99 Years." Unpublished typescript, c. 1968. Ragen Papers, box 4, ALL.

———. Scrapbooks. Ragen Papers, Joliet Area Historical Museum.

Ragen, Joseph E., and Charles Finston. *Inside the World's Toughest Prison.* Springfield IL: Charles C. Thomas, 1962.

Rector, Frank L. *Health and Medical Service in American Prisons and Reformatories.* New York: National Society of Penal Information, 1929.

Reimer, Hans. "Socialization in the Prison Community." *Proceedings of the Annual Congress of the American Prison Association* (1937), 151–55.

Rhodes, Lorna A. *Total Confinement: Madness and Reason in the Maximum Security Prison.* Berkeley: University of California Press, 2004.

Rosenberg, C. G., ed. *The Wonders of the World, Comprising Startling Incidents, Interesting Scenes, and Wonderful Events . . .* San Francisco: A. L. Bancroft, 1882.

Rubenstein, Bruce A., and Lawrence E. Ziewacz. *Three Bullets Sealed His Lips.* East Lansing: Michigan State University Press, 1987.

Rudow, Carl B. "Parties, Gambling, Rackets in Prison." *Detroit News*, July 24, 1945, 1–2.

Rules and Instructions for the Government of Inmates. Joliet: Stateville Penitentiary, [c. 1961].

Sabol, William J., et al. "Prison and Jail Inmates at Midyear 2006." *Bureau of Justice Statistics Bulletin*, June 2007.

Scudder, Kenyon J. *Prisoners Are People.* Garden City NY: Doubleday, 1952.

"Security of Custody and Segregation of Inmates at Jackson." October 7, 1952. G. Mennen Williams Papers, box 83, BHL.

Special Committee to Study the Michigan Department of Corrections. "The Michigan Prison Riots: Causal and Contributory Factors and Suggested Corrective Action." February 1953. G. Mennen Williams Papers, box 106, BHL.

Spectator, The. Inmate newspaper, State Prison of Southern Michigan.

Sykes, Gresham M. *The Society of Captives: A Study of a Maximum Security Prison.* Princeton: Princeton University Press, 1958, 1971.

Tannenbaum, Frank. *Osborne of Sing Sing.* Chapel Hill: University of North Carolina Press, 1933.

Tasker, Robert Joyce. *Grimhaven.* New York: Knopf, 1929.

Tocqueville, Alexis de, and Gustave de Beaumont. *On the Penitentiary System in the United States and Its Application in France.* Trans. Francis Lieber. Carbondale: Southern Illinois University Press, 1964.

Touhy, Roger, with Ray Brennan. *The Stolen Years.* Cleveland: Pennington, 1959.

Urdaburn, Johnny. "Chino: A City of Men, CIM U.S.A." In *Pioneer News: The Silver Anniversary of C.I.M.* (Chino CA: Pioneer News, 1966), 11.

Useem, Bert, and Peter Kimball. *States of Siege: U.S. Prison Riots, 1971–1986.* New York: Oxford University Press, 1991.

ValuSoft. Advertising material for Prison Tycoon. www.valusoft.com.

Warden's Files. Department of Corrections. AM.

Wetmore, S. W. "Life in a Great Prison." *Illustrated American* 1 (March 8, 1890), 58.

———. "The New System of Identification of Professional Criminals." *Frank Leslie's Illustrated Newspaper,* March 10, 1888, 55.

Wey, Hamilton. D. Physician's Report. *Twenty-First Year Book of the New York State Reformatory for the Fiscal Year Ending September 30, 1896.* Elmira: [Elmira Reformatory], 1897. Pp. 97–131.

Wilson, Donald Powell, and Harry Elmer Barnes. "A Riot Is an Unnecessary Evil." *Life,* November 24, 1952, 138–40, 142, 144, 147–48.

Wilson, George. "S.M.P. Laundry." *Spectator,* February 5, 1939, 6.

Wines, E. C. *The State of Prisons and of Child-Saving Institutions in the Civilized World.* Cambridge: Cambridge University Press, 1880.

Wood, Ike. *One Hundred Years at Hard Labor: A History of Marquette Prison.* Marquette MI: Ka-Ed, 1985.

Zimmerman, Saxe, and Zimmerman, Architects. *The New Illinois State Penitentiary at Stateville: A Treatise on Prison Design.* Springfield: State of Illinois, n.d.

Index

Index

51, 53; guard's memoir of, 183–
84; history of, 17, 18, 19, 21, 105,
121; homosexuality and, 84, 85,
92; inmate discipline and, 19–20,
121; population of, 5, 17, 108;
public image of, 2, 151; security
and, 108; tourists and, 2, 150;
uniforms at, 68, 69–70, 74; wardens' policies and, 108, 140–42,
149, 150, 153
social control. *See* discipline
solitary confinement, 18, 19, 120,
177
Southern Illinois Penitentiary
(Chester or Menard), 5, 22, 90
souvenirs, 3, 7, 9, 10
Speck, Richard, 106
Stateville (Ill.) Penitentiary, 64, 100,
177, 182, 183; administrative
image of, 151; administrative
problems of, 123–24; architecture of, 7, 30, 35, 36–41, 182;
cellhouse capacity of, 27; cell size
of, 49; convict gangs and, 169–70;
convict latitude and, 106, 123–
24, 167; convict number and, 70;
convict sex and, 82–83; convict
uniforms and, 64, 68, 72; deterio-
ration of, 172–73; homosexual inmates and, 82–83, 86, 106, 123;
opening of, 11; population of, 5,
196–97n1; public image of, 151;
Ragen's regime at, 123–27, 149,
150, 151, 154, 178, 197n1; Ragen's
successors at, 167; riot (1931) at,
124; riot (1973) at, 172; size of,
123; theory behind, 145, 151
Stevenson, Adlai, 163

striped uniforms, 66–68, 69, 72, 78–
79
strip-search, 46–47, 63–64
Stroud, Robert, 161–62
"supermax" prisons, 32, 177, 178
surveillance, 35, 40, 126, 127, 177
Sykes, Gresham M., 102
Symbionese Liberation Army, 170

"telephone pole" design, 33–34
television, 3, 15, 97, 143, 179–80,
183; Big House investigative report, 163; prison dome image
and, 24–25
Time (magazine), 149
Tocqueville, Alexis de, 19, 21
tourists, 2–3, 10, 15, 150, 181–82
transformation of persons, 11, 12,
46–48, 62–65, 67–68, 70–71, 74–
77, 90, 96, 97, 143, 146, 171, 179,
182
20,000 Years in Sing Sing (film), 70,
74, 99, 160

uniforms, 47–48, 62–74, 76–79; archetypal, 66–68; as civilian fashion influence, 79; film images of,
74, 76–79; Internet market for,
97; orange, 72; reformers and, 66,
68, 69, 72–73
utilitarianism, 152

victimless crimes, 175
visitors, 56–57, 63, 81

wall-less prisons, 8, 108, 164
wardens. *See* officers, prison
Warren, Earl, 153–54